Royal Horticultural Society

CONTAINER
GARDENING

Royal Horticultural Society

CONTAINER GARDENING

MITCHELL BEAZLEY

For Judith

RHS CONTAINER GARDENING

First published in Great Britain in 2013 by Mitchell Beazley,
an imprint of Octopus Publishing Group Ltd, Endeavour House,
189 Shaftesbury Avenue, London WC2H 8JY
www.octopusbooks.co.uk

An Hachette UK Company
www.hachette.co.uk

Published in association with The Royal Horticultural Society.

ISBN: 978 1 84533 588 5

A CIP record for this book is available from the British Library.

Set in Gill Sans and Minion.
Printed and bound in China.

Author Ian Hodgson
Publisher Alison Starling
Commissioning Editor Helen Griffin
Senior Editor Leanne Bryan
Copy-editor Joanna Chisholm
Proofreader Jane Birch
Indexer Helen Snaith
Art Director Jonathan Christie
Senior Art Editor Juliette Norsworthy
Designer Lizzie Ballantyne
Picture Research Manager Giulia Hetherington
Production Controller Allison Gonsalves
RHS Publisher Rae Spencer-Jones
RHS Editor Simon Maughan

Ian Hodgson is a garden writer and
designer, and former editor of *The
Garden* and editor-in-chief of RHS
journals for 18 years. Passionate about
all aspects of growing in containers,
he loves experimenting with new
ideas in his Cambridgeshire garden.

CONTENTS

• INTRODUCTION •

Growing plants in pots and other containers provides innumerable opportunities and rewards, irrespective of the size of your garden and especially if you have no garden at all. Little paved areas around doors and windows, or balconies and patios, can all be brought to life with just a few carefully chosen potted plants. Containers can make both an artistic and social statement, becoming focal points in their own right or just as contributors to the drama of the overall display. Foliage can be used to clothe and visually soften the impact of masonry, or help screen a view or fill a gap. Flowers add seasonal highlights, offering a bewildering range of colours and scents, while lifting your spirits.

GARDENS IN MINIATURE

Caring for potted plants is like gardening in miniature. It is an accessible way of testing your growing skills, while taking part in the cycles of life and the passing of the seasons. There are many ornamental plants suitable for all aspects and problem locations, from blistering sun to gloomy shade, or gusty, cold winds and harsh frosts. Even in the most challenging conditions you will be surprised just how decorative these plants can be and how well they will perform in containers if given a little care and attention. In the sunniest and most sheltered spot, you can grow in pots the most beautiful, exotic tender plants, such as passion flowers (*Passiflora*), bananas (*Musa*) and large-flowered hibiscus, that would just not survive long in the open garden in cool-temperate areas. Besides decorative displays, you can also grow some of your own food. While you might not become self-sufficient you will get a real sense of achievement, whether harvesting your own tomatoes, chillies or salads, picking your own herbs or plucking a crop of apples or figs.

ENCOURAGING CHILDREN

Growing in pots is also a good way of encouraging children to take their first steps in gardening. It is also easier for them to have a sense of ownership, particularly if they are given a pot to experiment with and can then see and appreciate the results of all their efforts. They will learn the basic skills and

*Gardens in miniature. Here tender evergreen blue potato bush (*Lycianthes rantonnettii*) is underplanted with dazzling annuals and perennials.*

Using containers is an easy and fun way to get children growing plants and observing nature.

(*Helianthus*) or gaudily toned dahlias. Tactile plants such as the velvety leaves of *Verbascum bombyciferum* or herbs such as sage (*Salvia*) or rosemary (*Rosmarinus*) will tempt little fingers to explore and experience everything on offer. Use fun plants such as the remarkable squirting cucumber (*Ecballium elaterium*), bizarrely shaped and brightly coloured squashes or try the large, smelly flowers of dragon arum (*Dracunculus vulgaris*).

techniques, such as planting or seed sowing, watering and feeding, training, trimming and harvesting, as well as discover the different life forms from trees to annuals, how they have become adapted to particular conditions, such as sun or shade, and how this influences their cultural needs. Use plants that are novel or have distinctive or interesting features to capture a child's imagination. Try visually arresting plants, such as brightly coloured sunflowers

By choosing crops that children like to eat you are also more likely to encourage them to grow their own, or you could show them how to make their very own salad mixtures.

Although self-evident, do take care with the plants that children are given to grow. Always show them what is edible and what is not, and avoid growing anything known to be an irritant or toxic, however beautiful or attractive. Research plant properties in books or on the internet.

ACCESSIBLE FOR ALL

For those who are infirm or unable to undertake the more strenuous aspects of gardening, container gardening offers a rewarding and easily accessible way to experience the fun and rewards of growing plants within levels of personal capability. Raised beds and planters or taller pots bring plants to a comfortable working height, ideal for those who are immobile or in wheelchairs (see p36). They can also be located near doorways or on patios to reduce the strain and inconvenience of having to walk any distance to garden. Pots on wheeled platforms can also be moved around to suit individual purposes or be relocated to better vantage points so they can be seen more clearly from the house.

No matter what your age or capability, container gardening really can be all things to all people, and it offers a way of growing plants that has many exciting possibilities.

Celebrate the seasons with creative combinations using ornamental plants or even decorative vegetables.

9

RULES & TOOLS

• WHERE TO START WITH CONTAINER-GROWN PLANTS •

The real attraction and appeal of container gardening is that in theory you can grow any plant your heart desires, even for a limited period and even if you have no access to garden soil at all. The bigger the ultimate size of the plant, the larger the pot required, although constraining roots and restricting feeding will keep plants in check. Some plants may be encouraged to flower more reliably when their roots are constrained: for example, many bulbs, such as African lily (*Agapanthus*), amaryllis (*Hippeastrum*) and veltheimia. You can also grow plants that may not tolerate or thrive in your normal soil conditions, such as acid-loving ericaceous plants – rhododendron, heather (*Erica*) – and fruit crops, such as blueberries.

With all plant forms now within your grasp you can choose to grow frost-tender exotics in heated conservatories, glasshouses or cold frames, or leave container-grown hardier plants in the open garden all year round.

The following provides an overview of all the types of plants you can grow and the points to bear in mind when you do.

Even if you have only a paved patio or balcony, containers offer numerous ways to grow and experience plants.

Trees & shrubs, including bonsai & topiary

Woody plants make imposing design statements year-round. Some trees, such as sweet bay (*Laurus nobilis*), look impressive when grown as a standard and the top clipped into a ball. Yew (*Taxus*) or box (*Buxus*) can also be clipped into formal shapes, such as

12

pyramids (see p160), or informally. The many cultivars of Japanese maples (*Acer japonicum*, *A. palmatum*) can be natural, trained or pruned as bonsai specimens.

Bamboos

For that oriental look try bamboo. In small spaces opt for bold, clump-forming *Sasa veitchii* or elegant *Shibataea kumasaca*. For dramatic effect in larger spaces use the black-stemmed bamboo *Phyllostachys nigra* or golden-stemmed *P. aurea*.

Herbaceous plants

Many perennials provide foliage and flower interest. In spring imposing *Euphorbia characias* is clothed in evergreen, linear leaves and yellow flowerheads. It makes a striking combination with pansies (*Viola × wittrockiana*) and spring bulbs, such as blue grape hyacinth (*Muscari*) and vibrant tulips (*Tulipa*).

Climbers

If you don't have space for a tree or shrub, grow a climber, such as clematis, up a wigwam of canes or an obelisk in a pot (see p150). In a sunny site use large-flowered, vibrant red *C.* 'Ville de Lyon', dark blue *C.* 'Polish Spirit' or small-flowered *C.* 'Pagoda'. In shade try demure, white *C.* 'Marie Boisselot' or pink-striped *C.* 'Nelly Moser'. Combine these with annual climbers, such as sweet peas (*Lathyrus odoratus*) for colour and scent.

Beautiful bedding

The choice of bedding plants is overwhelming, and plants can be grown on their own or in a supporting role. Pansies of various types are now available year-round in a range of self-colours or multicoloured patterns. Plant them with: winter bulbs, such as snowdrops (*Galanthus*) or aconites

13

PLANT SELECTION TIPS

- Grow plants that prefer the conditions that you can offer: for example, if you have a sunny site, grow sun-lovers; if a shady one, go for shade-loving plants.
- Choose plants that require minimal care and attention if you are not able to invest the required time and effort.
- Avoid plants that are overvigorous or need regular, long-term care, such as fast-growing trees, shrubs and climbers.

(*Aconitum*); spring plants, such as lungwort (*Pulmonaria*) or forget-me-not (*Myosotis*); tender summer shrubs, such as argyranthemum, osteospermum or penstemon; and autumn perennials, such as aster, chrysanthemum, or ice plant (*Sedum spectabile*).

Bulbs

While most bulbs are associated with spring, many others perform in early to midsummer. Try a generous clump of the ornamental onion *Allium hollandicum* 'Purple Sensation', with its globular, rich purple heads, underplanted with pink or blue petunia.

Succulents

Mix hardy succulents in shallow troughs or pans to enjoy their intriguing shapes, textures and colours. Try stonecrops (*Sedum*) or crassula, with their mats of creeping stems clothed with glaucous, globular leaves, or go for drosanthemum, with its vibrantly coloured flowers.

Alpines

Even the smallest spaces can fit in a collection of pots containing alpines

Highlight displays of evergreen perennials with seasonal bulbs and bedding.

(see p99). Many are easy to grow. Try silvery-leaved saxifrages (*Saxifraga*), which are covered with sheets of dainty pink, yellow or white flowers in spring, or the larger, shrubby rock roses (*Helianthemum*) studded with vibrant, often two-toned flowers, in rustic shades.

Water plants

Create your own aquatic garden with a tub or barrel lined with butyl rubber. Try marginal plants, such as dwarf bulrush (*Typha minima*) or Japanese iris (*Iris ensata*). In water at least 30cm (12in) deep use a dwarf waterlily, such as pale yellow *Nymphaea* 'Pygmaea Helvola'.

Vegetable crops

It's surprising how much you can grow to eat in containers. Breeding has created a host of mini-vegetables. Sunny patios are a haven for succulent cherry tomatoes, mini-aubergines and sweet and chilli peppers. Carrots and beetroot picked while young and succulent are easy to grow, and mixtures of various salads means you can make your own blends of leaves.

Fruit trees

Creating your own mini-orchard in pots can be a reality, not fantasy, thanks to

Small spaces are ideal for alpines, such as houseleeks (Sempervivum)*, which come in a wide range of textures and colours.*

rootstocks that keep trees dwarf and to new types of fruit bred for pots. You can soon be picking your own apples, pears, plums or the new plum–apricot crosses (see p59) with just a little know-how.

Herbs

This essential ingredient for so many dishes tastes so much better when picked fresh and used straight away. Why not grow combinations of herbs, such as rosemary (*Rosmarinus*) and sage (*Salvia*), to flavour your favourite foods?

• GETTING IT RIGHT
WITH CONTAINERS •

Potted displays of plants have the potential to make bold, imposing statements or add rich detail that will bring cohesion and drama to the garden. However, if overused or done carelessly, a confused and muddled mess can quickly ensue. To avoid this happening bear in mind the following points when planning arrangements.

POTS FIT FOR PURPOSE

Choosing the right receptacle for the job is an important part of the art and science of container cultivation. Practical considerations should always take precedence over style. Also, ensure the pot is robust and frost-resistant if it is to be retained outdoors in cold winters. The shape of the pot is important, too, especially with longer-term plantings; for this, avoid bulbous pots or narrow-necked Ali Baba jars. Pots need to be straight or with a direct taper to the base. Cost is also important. Spend the most on containers needed for the most prestigious positions, to show off both plant and pot. Use cheap, plastic ones for raising plants and veg or plant in growing bags and other durable plastic fabrics.

CONTAINERS IN DESIGN

How you position and distribute pots and other containers will strongly influence the visual appearance and character of their surroundings.

Use a single, large pot at the end of a pathway or vista or at the intersection of pathways, to form a focal point. It will also visually terminate the view.

Site a pair of matching pots and plantings either side of a door or pathway, to draw attention to an important feature, to frame a view or to demarcate a different type of space.

Single, large pots casually placed in a border can help break up planting and provide additional height and drama. Fill them with seasonal plants, which can be changed throughout the year, or use them to cover bare areas.

Group together pots of the same size, shape and colour alongside a path or up a flight of stairs to provide harmony and visual continuity. Place different sized pots in odd-numbered groups – three,

When used as an integral part of the design and chosen with care, containers can create dramatic effects in the garden.

Pairs of plantings placed at entrances or the ends of pathways will draw the eye and make imposing visual statements.

Place tender ornamentals, such as these jazzy amaranthus and gazania, in a sheltered, sunny spot by a window.

five or seven – with the tallest pot at the back and the smallest at the front. Alternatively, for a harmonious effect have the largest container in the centre, while for an eye-catching display offset the largest pot to the right or left so there is a sense of movement.

Site pots of plants next to seating areas or on patios to shelter the area or to enjoy exuberant, floral effects and scents. A group of pots filled with varied plantings will give a busier, more personal touch than a single, large pot – the effect will be more akin to a cottage garden than a formal setting.

POTS IN PROPORTION

Pots and other containers can be used to create a range of striking effects. A tall, narrow pot will make a confined space seem wider and raise the eye, particularly if used in isolation, perhaps set on a plinth to terminate a vista, or surrounded by low-growing plants. A squat or bulbous urn will provide an emphatic focal point. Urns exude a sense of classicism and period charm and if generously proportioned will give an impression of bounty and wellbeing, especially if allowed to overflow with plants. Those on stands or plinths add further grandeur and so attract greater attention but such urns need to be used sparingly. Save them for the most strategic points in the garden to retain their impact.

Always ensure a pot is of an appropriate size for its site; if too small, a pot set in a space of high significance will be overwhelmed and the sense of importance and high drama lost.

POT COLOUR & DESIGN

The colour and design of a pot exert a profound, visual impact on a setting.

Colour has the most immediate effect. Large, brightly coloured pots will vie for attention and give an illusion of being near, while dark, natural or neutral colours blend in more easily with the background or look further way. Therefore, use this powerful colour tool to full advantage when planning your planting schemes.

A successful restricted palette, here Tradescantia pallida *'Purpurea' in a weathered pot, often has a very powerful effect.*

Consider how colour will interact in your plantings. Strong colours dominate and will undermine the balance and visual impact of the scheme, unless you want shock contrasts in pure tones. Even so, use them carefully and sparingly to maximise the effect, otherwise the impact will be lost in a clashing riot of colour. To create balance and continuity in your planting schemes, link colours together, particularly strong ones, between your various containers. This is especially important if the pots frame an entrance or are placed at the ends of pathways.

Any patterning, texturing or embellishments to the surface of a container creates a more subtle but no less potent effect. Historical mouldings and embellishments, such as swags and gadroons, look best in period-style gardens, such as a country garden or parterre, while pots with clean, architectural and sculptured lines are better in a contemporary setting. A pot of inappropriate design will jar visually. Therefore, before buying a pot or pots, take swatches or test one out and be prepared to return it if its colour and design don't work.

PLANTING STYLES

Think about the character of the individual plants you might use. You may want to shape or train a permanent plant, such as a small tree, conifer or shrub, in some way to enhance the formal aspect of the garden or house or to contrast with a more relaxed planting. Alternatively, you may prefer to retain its natural habit so it harmonises with the surrounding planting or helps to soften a hard surface or other element of architecture. Plants with upright habits, such as yews (*Taxus*), other conifers and some broadleaved trees and shrubs, will accentuate narrow pots.

RIGHT PLANT, RIGHT PLACE

Choose plants that are most suitable for the prevailing conditions rather than trying to force plants to grow in positions alien to their needs. Fortunately, most pots can be turned or wheeled on trollies to better positions. When container-growing, be aware that soil can dry out rapidly, and moisture-loving

By marrying the style of pot to the type of planting you can further enhance atmosphere and mood.

20

This country-style planting is of an apricot English rose, white capparis, orlaya and red and yellow tickseed (Coreopsis).

kept watered and fed (see pp142, 146). This is usually a daily task when plants are in full growth and in flower. Most plants soon perish when exposed to prolonged drought. To avoid becoming a slave to the needs of your pot plants, have only as many as you can cope with and position containers so they are within easy reach. Avoid locating them out of sight and so out of mind.

NON-STOP CONTAINERS

Containers can be used year-round, and if they are carefully planned you can enjoy non-stop displays of flowers or even crop plants, such as leafy salads. Perhaps you want something different each season to ring the changes, adapting to the latest trends or reflecting the changing garden.

Create change around a permanent central feature plant, such as a tree or shrub, or climber on an obelisk. Group smaller containers to create rhythm and plant so foliage textures and colours create an overall balance, punctuated by flowers. Supplement supporting containers with seasonal bedding, or completely refresh them periodically with new plantings.

Always remove spent plants from the previous display, refresh the potting compost and add slow-release fertiliser.

plants will become stressed, wilt or die. Plants also need seasonal inputs of feed; they quickly outgrow their allotted space; and they often have bigger root systems than their leaf canopy above. The smaller the pot the more acute any problems become and the more vigilance you need to exercise.

CARING FOR PLANTS

Almost all types of plant, except perhaps drought-tolerant succulents, need to be

21

CONTAINER
BASICS

• WHAT CAN BE USED AS A CONTAINER? •

Containers can vary from the most expensive studio pottery and state-of-the-art, vertical growing systems for walls to *objets trouvés* and heavy-duty carrier bags. The controlling factors are the limit of your own imagination, personal taste and how much you want to pay.

All containers for growing plants must be durable enough for the period you want to grow the plants and sturdy enough to hold sufficient compost and moisture to sustain plant growth. If freestanding, the container must be sufficiently strong to hold the mature plant upright. Also important is the ability to allow excess water to seep away, usually via a number of drainage holes created in the base of the container.

The following are a selection of plant-appropriate container types, all of which have different practical advantages and disadvantages and aesthetic qualities.

When arranged in various sizes and textures, pots such as these Grecian-style urns can become features in themselves.

24

TERRACOTTA & GLAZED CLAY POTS

As well as being traditional and timeless in appearance, terracotta is heavy to lift and fragile if knocked. Ensure the clay is frost-resistant and crack-free before purchase.

Terracotta can be moulded into a range of shapes, with a variety of textures and decoration. Square shapes with classical swags are suitable for formal gardens.

Glazed terracotta pots hold moisture more effectively than unglazed ones. Select colours carefully so they don't overwhelm the planting scheme.

Strawberry pots have planting pockets around the sides. They can also be used for alpines, bulbs and small perennials.

NATURAL & MAN-MADE POTS

Containers moulded and shaped from natural minerals are the types most often used for permanent displays. Before the more widespread use of concrete in the late 19th century, pots and troughs were made from lead or timber or were chipped from stone or fired from moulded clay. Antique pieces can still be purchased for a price and look wonderful, but today antique reproductions in concrete or terracotta are so good it is difficult to tell old from new once they have aged for a few years. Those made of natural materials harmonise with the garden and weather and age to blend in with the garden scene. Pots with a coarser finish, such as concrete and stone, quickly become colonised by mosses and lichens, further adding to the sense of gentle decay. This natural colonisation can be encouraged by painting the surface of the pots with natural yogurt (see box on p154).

Stone

All stone containers are heavy to move, and depending on their thickness are also fragile to varying degrees if bumped or dropped. Their thick construction provides good insulation, protecting roots from scorching in summer and frost damage in winter.

Terracotta

This is the most fragile, natural plant-pot material. The porous clay absorbs moisture, and the alternating freeze/thaw of winter weather exerts enormous pressures, causing cracking of the pot, often around the rim, which quickly crumbles. Therefore, when buying terracotta for use outdoors, ensure it is guaranteed frost-resistant; many such pots are not.

The porous characteristic of unglazed terracotta means that moisture is lost over the whole pot surface, so it tends to dry out more quickly than pots made from other materials. It may need watering more frequently, too, especially when small. This does not happen with glazed terracotta pots. Note that unglazed pots can be lined with plastic, if necessary.

PITHOI & URNS

Pithoi are the large ceramic storage vessels from Greece, particularly Crete, used since ancient times to hold oil and other liquids. Today original pieces are imported for use as decorative pieces for the garden and look stunning as a focal point in a Mediterranean-style garden. However, they are usually waisted or bulbous in shape and, being taller than

---

URNS & WOODEN CONTAINERS

Urns are imposing features traditionally made from terracotta, cast iron or lead, but are now manufactured from lighter aluminium alloy or plastic.

Versailles planters are ideal for exhibiting clipped topiary and are useful where formality is required. They are generally made in wood, and larger models sometimes have detachable side panels.

Half-barrels are useful for growing small trees and shrubs, but are heavy and cumbersome. If the wood is allowed to dry out, the barrel may fall apart.

wide, are best used on their own rather than for growing plants. The durability and frost-resistance are not always known. While originals are expensive, modern replicas are cheaper and likely to be more resistant in cool-temperate areas.

Urns are traditionally goblet- or chalice-shaped receptacles, frequently with a short stem and a foot and can be set on a pedestal; they are often decorated in relief. Size and shape can vary, and some are raised on plinths, adding to their dramatic appearance. Chalice-shaped urns have a wider mouth than goblets, but a shallower basin and so can accommodate large plants only in the centre. They are prone to dry out quickly, particularly around the rim. On balance, the goblet shape is better for supporting plants.

VERSAILLES PLANTERS

These traditional planters are unsurpassed for their chic, formal look, and they were named after the famous French garden in which they were first used. The cubed frame carcass is inset with interlocking slatted side panels, which in smaller sizes are fixed in position. Larger types, to 1.2m (4ft) across, can traditionally be dismantled and re-erected where required.

WOODEN CONTAINERS

Wooden containers have long been popular in gardens. Timber is largely fashioned into angular geometric shapes, usually as cubes or troughs, although multisided containers such as octagons can be found. Construction can be jointed and glued manually (generally expensive), while factory-produced pots usually include brackets, screws, nails or glue and can be bought ready-made or as self-assembly kits. Always check the construction carefully as cheap assembly systems generally end up falling apart after a season or two.

Raised timber planters help gardeners to grow their own crops conveniently at waist height, and are also excellent for those who cannot bend or crouch. These often come with a range of accessories and canopies to protect plants from excess sun, wind and insect pests.

Oak barrels

Old oak barrels are a traditional favourite and ideal where a more relaxed style is required. They are good for large, massed ornamental displays or growing vegetables. Being wider than high, oak barrels are very stable and excellent for small trees and shrubs with surface roots, such as rhododendron,

Japanese maples (*Acer japonicum, A. palmatum*) and magnolia.

Although durable, these barrels will slowly rot, particularly through the base and so the surfaces are often charred or painted to help provide further protection. The spars of the barrel must remain damp to be watertight and so work best if kept filled with damp compost. For potted water gardens protect barrels with a butyl pond liner.

METAL CONTAINERS

Lead and copper containers have long been used to store water, but these metals are currently experiencing a renaissance, with all manner of contemporary designs available. Many period and vintage metal receptacles, such as old cisterns, old washtubs, tin baths and galvanized buckets, can be converted into planting containers. Ensure these have sufficient drainage holes and that ferrous (iron/steel-based) containers are galvanized on the inside (to protect against damp soil) and beneath (to prevent rust from staining any hard surface on which the container stands).

Sheet metal containers with galvanized or copper finishes are ideal for contemporary gardens. Their various shapes and designs will provide a utilitarian or minimalist look. However, avoid any that have an inner metal skin with no drainage holes, as such holes would be difficult to drill yourself.

METAL & PLASTIC CONTAINERS

Forged and sculpted metal can provide a Victorian or rustic look in the garden, particularly when allowed to rust naturally.

Light, robust and durable, plastic is the most widely used material for containers, and when sensitively moulded and coloured can emulate terracotta.

Large plastic pots are practical, strong and ideal for growing collections of fresh herbs and vegetables.

The main problem with metal containers is that they conduct heat quickly in sun, and in prolonged heat can 'cook' roots and damage plants, particularly those in smaller pots. In winter they also offer little insulation from hard frosts. A disadvantage of lead is that it is very heavy, somewhat fragile and very easily marked.

PLASTIC & FIBREGLASS POTS

Plastics and composites are now the most widely used materials for plant containers. Modern plastics are flexible, lightweight, impact resistant and possess high tensile strength. They are also stabilized against damage from strong sunlight and extreme temperatures. Sophisticated moulding and coloration and high-quality finishes have facilitated sensitive mimicking of other materials, such as timber, metal or stone.

Fibreglass is used to create a wide variety of plant containers, particularly troughs and tubs. The fibre is fashioned around a mould and bound together with a resin filler. The result is a strong, lightweight, water- and weatherproof

material that is capable of taking various finishes and is fairly impact resistant.

Resin technology has also improved dramatically, and resins are used on their own or in conjunction with other materials to bind them or create particular effects. Resins are highly weather and impact resistant and have long-term durability. Being expensive they tend to be utilised for premium-priced products.

There is widespread concern that most plastics and other similar products do not decay, which could pose a long-term threat to planet Earth. Biodegradable plastics, however, are made (see p32).

SINKS & HYPERTUFA

When used creatively and sited with care, Belfast or butler sinks can be a real asset to the container garden, especially if a number are positioned together in different orientations and heights to create a really attractive feature. They are often a home for miniature alpines such as rock jasmine (*Androsace*), encrusted saxifrages (*Saxifraga*), heron's bill (*Erodium*) and small bulbs as well as dwarf conifers, but can be used to grow other plants too, such as hardy carnivorous plants. These sinks are usually set on brick or stone piers to raise them off the ground and make tending plants easier. Ensure they are level or with a slight fall to the plug hole to allow excess moisture to escape.

The glossy white, ceramic finish on a sink can look stark in the garden, unless you are trying to achieve a modern, minimalist style. Many people therefore paint them with a masonry paint (you may need to apply a render first to enable it to stick) or cover them by what is known as 'hypertufa', a mixture of mortar and coir. This hardens to create a rustic, stone-like mantle, which soon mellows, eventually becoming colonised by mosses and lichens.

IMPROVISED CONTAINERS

When container gardening you have a great opportunity to innovate and convert all manner of domestic or industrial objects into makeshift containers. Objects are recycled that would otherwise be disposed of. If chosen wisely and carefully, you can add distinctive character and/or humour to the look and style of your garden and you can also save money. You need to marry the size and proportion of the plant to the container. Small plants, such as alpines,

Containers of all kinds can be used to grow plants as long as they hold the potting compost and allow water to drain.

IMPROVISED CONTAINERS

Utensils such as old teapots with holes drilled into the base provide quirky containers for plants such as alpines or succulents.

Chimney pots can be planted up by either filling the trunk with compost and then planting, or by setting a potted plant in the top of the chimney.

Chimney pots make imposing features either used singly or in groupings. Original chimney pots are terracotta, but plastic facsimiles are also available.

Turn old boots into a talking point by packing them with potting compost and planting summer bedding and other creeping plants.

small bulbs and groundcover plants, can be grown in old boots and other footwear or in shallow trays, while larger plants can be accommodated in old beer crates or orange boxes, or stacks of old tyres. Where appearance is less important and only a temporary solution is required, many more articles can be put to good use. Stout carrier bags or old compost bags can be trimmed down and used to grow vegetables for a season. To prevent them toppling over, stack three carrier bags against each other.

BIODEGRADABLE CONTAINERS

Containers made from recycled materials or from natural or synthetic products that biodegrade or decompose are becoming increasingly important in gardening. They currently are best for the propagation and raising of young plants. There are simple devices to make cells from old newspaper (ideal for raising vegetables), through to pots woven from coir fibre (which are more natural-looking for water plants than a plastic mesh basket).

On a more sophisticated level there are decorative containers made from rice or shredded bamboo husk bound together with a natural resin, which starts to degrade after three to five years. Some are coloured with vegetable dyes to make them more decorative. All are more expensive than plastic, but this may change as their use becomes more widespread and costs of production are reduced.

Biodegradable plastics are now available, but they disintegrate into smaller particles instead of decaying completely after a number of years.

When suitably lined, mesh gabions can be used to grow ornamentals, vegetables and strawberries.

GABIONS

Although more usually found in the construction industry as retaining walls or to stabilize shorelines, you can also use these rubble-filled cages to grow plants. Plant them with alpines and other dwarf plants by systematically packing the sides with rock and then filling the centre with potting compost, usually John Innes No 1 rather than a peat-free multipurpose one. Tuck the plants into the rocks so their roots bed into the compost as you build up the sides. A gabion is heavy, so construct it in its final position.

For a lighter alternative, line the gabion with landscape fabric or capillary matting, overlapping the edges to create a seal and then fill it with potting compost. Cut a small cross in the fabric, and tuck the plants through the hole so the roots bed into the compost.

Gabions can also be used to create a seated planter. Either use two cubes pushed together or a single rectangular basket. Plant up the sides and then position slats or planking across the top of the gabion, wiring these to the basket to provide the seat.

• HANGING BASKETS •

Hanging baskets and bowls have long been popular containers for floral displays or growing food in spaces that would otherwise have remained under-utilised or completely wasted (see box on p165). The larger the basket the more self-sustaining it is, with regard to watering. Baskets should be no less than 20cm (8in) wide, and ideally 30cm (12in) wide.

LINING BASKETS

These hemispherical, galvanized or chrome-plated mesh bowls are traditionally lined with live sphagnum or other types of moss (see p167). While this looks really attractive, there is widespread concern about the continued sourcing of live moss from the wild, so instead use any durable, porous fabric that can be easily cut to insert the plants. Try, for example, manufactured or recycled liners (see p163).

WATER RESERVOIRS

Many commercial hanging baskets contain a circle of impervious material in the centre to act as a water reservoir to

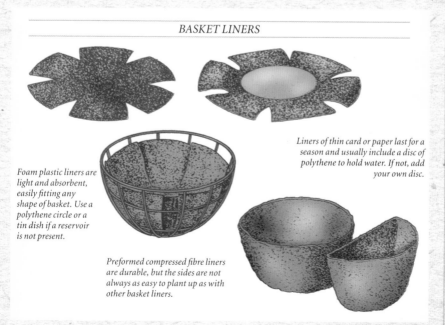

BASKET LINERS

Foam plastic liners are light and absorbent, easily fitting any shape of basket. Use a polythene circle or a tin dish if a reservoir is not present.

Liners of thin card or paper last for a season and usually include a disc of polythene to hold water. If not, add your own disc.

Preformed compressed fibre liners are durable, but the sides are not always as easy to plant up as with other basket liners.

prevent water running out the bottom of the basket. If this is not present, set a tinfoil pie dish in the base of the basket to act as a water reservoir.

PLASTIC BOWLS

As you can plant only the surface of a plastic bowl, this curtails the possibility of producing a dramatic ball of foliage and flower. Being solid sided, it holds moisture well, so is less apt to dry out. Some models have integral reservoir systems (see p163).

SPECIAL CONCERNS

Many composts for bowls and baskets include water-retaining gels to conserve moisture. You can also buy gel separately

These cockscomb (Celosia) and French marigolds (Tagetes patula) make an elevated, eye-catching combination.

and mix this into the potting compost before planting (see box on p139).

Fully laden hanging baskets and bowls are tremendously heavy, so it is essential that all fixings and hangings can support the weight placed on them. Brackets should have adequate bracing and be soundly secured to a solid surface (see p168). Simple hook eyes threaded into fascia boards are insufficient anchorage.

There are various devices to help watering, such as extendable lances and retractable line devices that enable you to raise and lower the container.

WATERING HANGING BASKETS

Extendable lances with swivel-headed attachments enable you to target water directly into the basket.

Use a hose on a low flow rate for baskets you can reach; high flows will displace the compost.

A watering can with a long spout is an option, but it is heavy and time-consuming to use.

• RAISED BEDS •

Raised beds can offer all the benefits of container growing and more. They:

● Provide a layer of fertile soil over an existing one that may be impoverished or difficult to cultivate.

● Can be used to establish a growing zone over a paved or impervious area of hard standing.

● Provide particular soil or environmental growing conditions to support specific types of plant that may not tolerate existing soil conditions.

● Elevate plants so that particular types, such as alpines, can be observed more closely.

● Facilitate easier working by raising plants up to a convenient height.

Beds need be no more than 15cm (6in) deep and 1.2m (4ft) wide to facilitate working easily from both sides. Also allow space for access around the bed.

A raised bed can be of real benefit for those with no soil to grow plants or who have difficulty kneeling or bending.

NO-DIG BEDS

Raised beds have helped stimulate wider interest in the technique of no-dig cultivation. This involves improving the soil by spreading a layer of well-rotted garden compost or manure on the surface of the bed in late autumn and allowing it to be worked into the soil by worm activity. Sowing and tending crops also helps aerate the surface layers.

RETAINING MATERIALS

Railway sleepers, nailed together, can be used to form a basic raised bed. Always choose brand-new ones and treat them with a clear preservative; avoid any covered in creosote or tar. For a more rustic garden atmosphere, go for stout, hazel wattle panels or logs. For a country garden style, use rough-hewn or dressed rock to create a dry stone wall or try reconstituted concrete blocks, many of which have delightful textures and finishes in a range of colours. Leave pockets for plants, such as rock roses (*Helianthemum*) or ferns, or encourage native plants to colonise soil-laden

PROFILE OF A RAISED BED

These elevated structures are filled with potting compost or garden soil over a generous layer of drainage materials, enabling cultivation over any ground.

fissures. Choose second-hand, hard-burnt, frost-resistant brick for a more urban-look raised bed, which can be constructed rough or fully mortared. Depending on the size and extent of a brick-walled raised bed, it may need foundations on which to bed the bricks. Engage the services of a professional builder if the wall is more than 60cm (2ft) high. Leave weep holes every 60cm (2ft) or so on the sides, for excess moisture to escape, and include a damp-proof course of engineering brick or plastic or bitumised fabric and a durable coping to shed water. Render the inside of each wall with water-proof masonry paint to prevent water seepage and staining of the front face of the bricks.

• WINDOWBOXES & TROUGHS •

Nothing surpasses the appearance of a well-planted windowbox thronging with perky spring bulbs or festooned by a skirt of summer flowers and foliage. The generous sills of a period Victorian or Edwardian house can accommodate a windowbox on the sill itself, while more

modern properties, with their narrower windowsills, should have such a planter suspended beneath the sill, securely bracketed to the wall.

PRACTICAL CONSIDERATIONS

Windowboxes and troughs can be made from plastic, timber or galvanized sheet metal. Sometimes there may be a decorative outer shell into which fits a trough, which can be removed when a planting display is over and replaced with the new plants. The wider and deeper the container, the more root room and the better the resulting growth and floral display. Ideally, they should be no less than 15cm (6in) high

As they are long and narrow, troughs can fit into otherwise difficult sites, such as windowsills and wall tops.

and wide. Narrow containers are apt to dry out quickly, particularly when facing full sun.

Wall fixings for windowboxes and troughs must be securely fixed and strong enough to provide support when fully laden. Loose fixings usually result in disaster. Use small brackets to hold each windowbox in place. This is particularly important if it is positioned at any great height when slippage could be dangerous. To reduce weight, fill such planters with loamless potting compost.

• GROWING BAGS
& COLLAPSIBLE PLANTERS •

Growing bags offer an inexpensive way to cultivate many crops, particularly shallow-rooting ones or those with restricted root systems such as salads, tomatoes, cucumbers and melons. They come in various depths. The deeper ones are suitable for longer-term crops and those with questing root systems as they contain more potting compost.

The manufacturer's label usually indicates how many of each plant type can be supported in that bag; often, it is three tomato or cucumber plants per bag. Loosen the compost before cutting the panels where each plant is to be inserted. Always retain some linking strips across the bag for stability and to prevent the bag from slumping, thus making it difficult to water.

Growing bags are usually perforated to allow excess moisture to escape, but if no holes seem present make some in the underside of the bag with a fork before use, or snip off the corners of the bag.

COLLAPSIBLE PLANTERS
A development of the growing bag are collapsible troughs and other planters,

---

CUCUMBERS IN GROWING BAGS

Raise plants from seed in late spring and grow on in 10cm (4in) pots until 2–4 leaves have formed. Then plant three cucumbers per growing bag and water in.

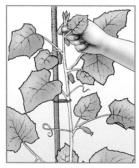

Support the cucumber vine with a stout bamboo cane or a network of wires secured into the glasshouse framework or other structure if growing outdoors.

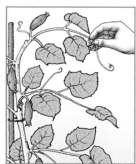

Pinch out the tip when the vine reaches the top of the support. Keep the cucumbers evenly moist, feed regularly and harvest fruit as and when it is ready.

measuring 45cm (18in) by 75cm (30in), made from woven polypropylene fabric. If practicality is more important than appearance then they are good value for money. These troughs are 30cm (12in) deep and so offer a much deeper root run than growing bags. They are therefore ideal for roots crops such as carrots, beetroot and salad potatoes as well as small plantations of field crops such as dwarf French beans. Because of their size, the compost remains moist for longer in such troughs.

To prevent it collapsing, bamboo canes are inserted through sleeves at the margins of the trough or through strips of fabric sown across it.

GROWING BAG COMPOSTS

The compost in a growing bag is ready to use. Traditionally, the growing medium was finely milled peat compost. Due to concern about peat use, however, alternative products and their blends are now available, including coir or milled coconut fibre/husk, pulverised softwood and composted green waste. Fertiliser and water-retaining gels are also often included.

Many manufacturers are now promoting the ingredients used in their compost more visibly, and schemes such

Bottomless pots (termed ring culture) bedded into growing bags creates additional growing space for crops such as tomatoes.

as the Growing Media Initiative between the trade and other bodies, such as the RHS, are working towards the complete removal of peat from general potting compost by 2020 (see p136).

Whichever type of potting compost you choose, ensure that it is fresh stock and has not been spoilt by storing outdoors to become wet and soggy.

ROOT SPACE

Establish young plants initially in pots 13cm (5in) or less in diameter, so they have good root systems before being planted in the growing bag. Alternatively, you can sow directly into a growing bag; this is especially suitable for leafy salad crops as you can use thinnings as they grow. To make it easier for the roots of young seedlings to grow, cover the surface of the bag's compost with a proprietary seed compost and sow into this finer soil.

For stem-rooting crops such as tomatoes or cucumbers, use an old technique called 'ring culture'. Here a bottomless 27–30cm (9–12in) pot is bedded into the bag, half- to three quarters-filled with compost in which young plants are established. This provides extra room for surface roots, allowing others to quest deeper, and a container in which to more easily apply water and liquid feed.

Tall plants in growing bags require firm support via bamboo canes or one of the various frame kits on the market.

Products are available to help when watering a growing bag. These range from reservoir bags with trickle or drip irrigation to plastic collars that fit round the base of the plant and are bedded into the bag. The water-holding collars seep moisture directly into the growing bag.

SUPPORT FRAMES

A number of freestanding framework systems are available to provide support for plants in growing bags. Alternatively, bags can be placed near canes or plastic mesh secured to walls or freestanding frameworks. When growing under glass, fix the canes and wires to the framework.

• WALL GROWING SYSTEMS & PLANTERS •

As gardens become progressively smaller, all available vertical space, such as walls and fences, cries out to be utilised. Thankfully, there has been a leap forward in the technologies available to gardeners to allow them to do just that. The simplest are bags or planting pouches fashioned from woven polypropylene fabric, felt or thick polythene. They may comprise a single, large pouch or a series of smaller ones, which hang down like streamers. These are secured and slung from stout fencing, fence posts, chain-link fencing or walls. The pouches can be watered by hand or from drip irrigation systems. They are designed to sustain plants for a year; they should then be cleaned and replenished with fresh compost and food if they are to be reused.

Ensure fence panels are strong enough to withstand the significant additional loading from such a wall growing system and that the planting pouches are fixed securely to supporting structures. Bear in mind that water running out of pouches can stain the supporting surface.

Growing systems for greening walls offer opportunities to plant a range of evergreen perennials.

FURTHER OPTIONS

Another neat solution is fixing systems that enable standard-shaped plant pots, 10–13cm (4–5in) or less in diameter, to be attached to drainage pipes, walls and fence posts. Also look out for specially designed bracket systems that enable hanging baskets conveniently to be attached to fence posts.

Compost-filled, fabric or polythene pouches offer one of the simplest methods of growing plants on vertical surfaces.

GREEN WALLS

In recent years, sophisticated systems have come onto the market to create the so-called 'living' or 'green wall'. These are the 'self-sustaining' plant communities, normally composed of hardy evergreen perennials – often groundcover plants – that are massed together for decorative effect and sustained in a growing medium, which provides a continual supply of moisture and essential nutrients.

Products usually come as integrally moulded units, which are then linked to cover the space. Each unit contains a number of hoppers into which the plants and growing medium are placed. The hoppers are carefully designed to maintain moist root conditions without becoming waterlogged. A pump transports water (including liquid feed) to the top of the installation. It then percolates down using gravity via a system of canals and portals linked to each plant in the hopper or via a system of drip or trickle irrigation nozzles. Some systems may link to capillary matting. Computer monitoring enables moisture and feed levels to be carefully controlled.

The better systems also allow surplus water and feed to be collected and reused. As these are expensive, such a green wall system is only worth considering when integral with a carefully considered design, rather than as an afterthought.

CROPS IN
CONTAINERS

• WHICH CROPS CAN YOU GROW? •

The ability to grow your own food is a rewarding and exciting experience. Harvesting fresh food straight from the garden, when you know precisely how it has been grown and it is at the peak of perfection, is one of life's real pleasures. More importantly, however, it has a critical role to play in the wellbeing of both humans and the planet. With a little know-how and planning you can grow herbs, almost all vegetables and many types of fruit in pots.

HERBS APLENTY

All herbs are easily grown in containers, where you can provide the warm, well-drained conditions that most of them like (see p58). Some are best raised as annuals each year; others are perennial, while other herbs are shrubby or bulbous (as in chives and other onion relatives).

VERSATILE VEGETABLES

Cultivating your own food is not only liberating but also, with a little experience and trial and error, you can grow and harvest crops in ways that might not be available in supermarkets or greengrocers. For example, you can pick vegetables, such as carrots or beetroot, when immature (when they are often sweeter and more succulent), or use parts of the vegetable normally discarded, but still nutritious. Leaves of beetroot, or pea shoots and tendrils, offer interesting textures and colours, while the piquant seed pods of radishes can be added to salads, soups and stir-fries. The flowers of many vegetables can also be used as an edible garnish. The range of vegetables suitable for intensive cultivation in pots and raised beds has substantially increased in recent years.

BEST CROPS

Vegetables

- Beetroot
- Compact cucumbers
- Chilli and sweet peppers
- Dwarf French beans
- Potatoes
- Salad greens
- Salad onions
- Tomatoes

Fruit

- Apples
- Apricots
- Blueberries
- Figs
- Gooseberries
- Grapes
- Jostaberry
- Pears
- Plums
- Strawberries

POTTED FRUIT

In the confines of a container some fruit crops are much more productive and easier to grow and care for than others. In practice, the smaller the fruit plant the more productive it will be. Strawberries, blueberries and gooseberries, for example, will all do well in containers; gooseberries even tolerate some shade and drought.

Top fruit, such as apples and pears (see p59), and stone fruit, such as peaches and nectarines, require large

Attractive as well as edible; site fruiting crops such as peppers, tomatoes, and strawberries in prominent, sunny positions.

pots. Fortunately, the techniques of growing them in this way compared with plants in the open ground are easily learned. Dwarfing rootstocks, reliable, disease-resistant and self-fertile cultivars and appropriate care all play a part in enabling you to grow your own fruit without needing garden space for a full-size tree.

• VEGETABLES IN POTS •

Some vegetables have long been associated with container cultivation, particularly those tender crops generally grown in glasshouses in cool-temperate areas, such as tomatoes, cucumbers, melons, peppers and aubergines. Here, breeders have produced cultivars that are more compact and more durable for cultivation outdoors in often fickle summers; the plants are also resistant to the devastating diseases they are likely to encounter when grown outdoors.

Other vegetable crops are ideal for pot culture for the following reasons:

● They are standard cultivars, but can be harvested when young or immature.

● The height/proportions of the plant has been reduced so it is more manageable in a pot or small space.

CONTAINER CHOICES

The type of container required will depend on the vegetable you want to grow, whether it is a taprooted crop (such as carrots), a leafy salad crop (such as lettuces) or a shrubby or climbing plant (such as peppers, tomatoes or cucumbers). You may also want your vegetables to become a feature in themselves. Many have attractive flowers, leaves or fruit and can be collectively grown for display. If long-lived, such as rainbow-leaved chard, the vegetable can be used as an incidental element with other ornamental plants. In this instance you will want an aesthetically attractive container, such

No space or suitable container should be overlooked to exploit any opportunity to grow your own fresh food.

When planting a larger container with climbing beans, add a few sweet peas (Lathyrus odoratus) for cut flowers.

as a terracotta urn, moulded plastic tub or timber crib or planter, rather than a purely functional growing bag, black-plastic pot or recycled container.

PLANNING YOUR CROPS

Vegetables have different rates of growth, and, depending on whether they are harvested for their roots, stems, leaves or fruit, these will determine how and when they should be grown. The way plants produce their edible parts is also influential. Some crops can be selectively picked over a period of time, while others are completely removed when mature. For example, tomatoes and cucumbers are grown for the whole summer and their fruit picked as it ripens; Swiss chard leaves, too, are removed as required, while hearting lettuces are usually harvested in their entirety before they bolt.

It is essential you plan your vegetable campaign in advance to help ensure you maximise the yield from your various containers and maintain continuity of cropping, particularly if you want to mix various vegetables together. The

good news about container cultivation is that you don't have to worry about growing in a rotation, that is, you do not need to change the position of various vegetable types each year as you would in open ground, to prevent the build-up of damaging pests and diseases.

Ensure you use fresh potting compost in your containers each year. After you have finished, place old, spent compost on the compost heap or dig it into the ground as a soil conditioner.

CROPPING PLANS

The easiest method of growing vegetables is to have just one type of crop per container, be it lettuces, beetroot or carrots. Here you can provide perfect conditions for the crop and replace it with another once it has been harvested.

With a little ingenuity, you can mix tall crops with shorter or more compact types: for example, you could have a tomato or cucumber in the centre and underplant this with various salad plants or baby beetroot. Later crops, such as runner beans, planted out in early summer, could be preceded by a catch crop of radishes or spring onions.

If you require a plantation of a vegetable such as dwarf French beans or dwarf peas, use a woven fabric vegetable planter (see p39), as it combines a good surface area in which to plant with an appropriate depth for the roots.

CHOOSING VARIETIES

While you should always grow crops for their flavour or other culinary qualities, where possible select those cultivars that have been bred in your own country as they will better withstand any variable weather and particular diseases. An ever-widening selection of tomatoes, cucumbers, aubergines and sweet peppers can now be purchased as young plants grafted on rootstocks that are tolerant of colder soil conditions than

previously; these also offer resistance to soil-borne diseases. This enables plants to establish quickly and start growth and cropping earlier, particularly outdoors. Cropping is further extended into autumn, when conditions start to cool once again.

Both tomatoes and potatoes are being bred for improved resistance to late blight, which in warm, humid summers can devastate crops.

GROWING CONDITIONS

To give their best results, vegetable crops require consistency in the quality of their growing conditions. Place your containers in as sheltered a position as possible, but where they will receive good light for a large portion of the day. Avoid areas exposed to strong or cold winds, which will check growth and cause damage to the plants.

Clustering crop containers together helps provide protection, creating a microclimate of humid air and mutual shade, as well as the convenience of having plants all in one place.

Crops such as tomatoes, aubergines, sweet and chilli peppers require bright sunshine to ripen swelling fruit and improve flavour and sweetness. If located in a hot position, do not allow

Plan pots of vegetables in advance to provide a succession of produce, and use dwarf cultivars bred for containers.

plants to dry out. In severe conditions, such as burning sun or torrential rain, shade crops with a sheet of horticultural fleece to prevent damage.

Keep plants evenly moist (see p142), because unbalanced conditions of drought and waterlogging affects performance and causes uneven ripening and physical damage to fruit crops, like tomatoes and sweet peppers.

Feed leafy salad crops and young fruit crops every week with liquid nitrogen fertiliser (see p146). Once fruit crops start to flower, change to high-potash liquid fertiliser, such as tomato food.

SUPPORTING CROPS

Vine-like crops require support. Tomatoes can be tied to stout bamboo canes, while twining climbers, such as cucumbers, runner beans, peas and mangetout, need more elaborate support systems (see p150). For a single cucumber you could use trellis supported by a cane (see p39), or for multiple plants create a tepee of canes, which fit inside the pot rim. Shorter varieties of peas can be encouraged to clamber over short lengths of brushwood inserted between the plants. Climbing crops in pots can also be trained up trellis or sweet-pea netting attached to a wall or fence.

To maximise the space why not combine different types of climber? Mixing together varieties of beans

with different flower colours makes a very attractive feature, especially if you include a sweet pea or two as well.

SOURCING PLANTS

For some high-value crops, particularly those for glasshouse cultivation in cool-temperate areas (such as tomatoes, cucumbers, sweet and chilli peppers, aubergines and melons), you can choose between growing from seed or purchasing young plants grown in plugs of potting compost. When you want only a few plants, particularly if grafted, then purchasing young plants is

Cherry or smaller-fruited cultivars offer greatest reliability for ripening tomatoes outdoors in cool-temperate areas.

the better option even though it is more expensive. Remove plants from their outer and inner transparent packaging as soon as you can after arrival in your home and pot each one into a 7.5–10cm (3–4in) container (see p81).

SEED SOWING

There are two sowing techniques, each suitable for some crops more than others. The first is pre-sowing in plug or celltrays, or in small pots, to raise your own plantlets and then planting out to final spacings. The second technique is to sow directly into the final containers.

Celltray sowing

Sow in plastic plug or celltrays for easier management of seedlings than those in individual 7–7.5cm (2½–3in) pots. Fill the plugs or cells with peat-free seed compost, water it and then sow seeds singly, if easily handled, or else insert 2–4 seeds per plug or cell (see box on p124). Keep the compost moist and maintain the minimum temperature required for germination. See the individual seed packets for instructions.

After sowing, place the celltrays or pots in a glasshouse or cold frame to provide frost protection in spring for the seedlings; a temporary plastic structure will also do this job. You could make your own cold frame out of timber decking nailed to uprights, with a plastic or Perspex top to let light in.

If sown in small groups, thin out weaker seedlings as plants expand, to leave just one. When fully established, harden plants off by gradually exposing them to outdoor temperatures. Then plant out to their final spacing, which for salad crops and leaf vegetables could be slightly closer than usual if you plan to start harvesting before fully mature.

53

Use celltrays for raising vegetables, either by sowing directly in each cell or growing on individual seedlings.

Sprinkle seeds of crops, such as cut-and-come-again salads, over deeper trays of compost to mature in situ.

POTTED POTATOES

Although the number of tubers produced
will be small, grow potatoes in pots if you
have thin, dry soil or a build-up of soil-
borne diseases, or don't have a garden. Use
any container 20–30cm (8–12in) or more
deep and 30cm (12in) wide, with drainage
holes. Select early or maincrop varieties,
which have small but prolific tubers, or try
coloured heritage or unusual salad types.
For a late or Christmas crop use a blight-
resistant cultivar. The number of tubers
needed depends on pot width: use five in
a 60cm (24in) pot; two or three in a 45cm
(18in) one. If you can give protection, plant
from late winter, otherwise wait till early
spring, finishing in midsummer.

Direct sowing

This technique is just like sowing
vegetables in the open ground, except
that the seed is sown directly into
the container or growing system.
Traditionally, seeds are sown in straight
lines set a certain distance apart, to allow
the crop to develop optimally. However,
container crops can be grown at closer
spacings, particularly if harvested when
immature or if they are dwarf cultivars.
Sowings can also be made to suit the
shape and size of the container: for
example, radishes, dwarf beets or spring
onions could be sown around the edge
or in small patches to fill a gap between
established plantings. Mixtures of salad
leaves for single harvest or cut-and-
come-again ones can be broadcast sown,
spacing seed evenly to cover the surface
or else in patches or in lines.

Growing bags (see p39) can also be
sown directly with a range of crops.
Lightly firm the growing bag surface to
create a seedbed. If the compost is too
coarse to create this, cover the surface with

seed compost and sow into this. Water the seeds in and cover the container with a layer of horticultural fleece to maintain heat and humidity and to protect seeds and seedlings from birds and vermin. Once seedlings emerge, continue to protect with fleece at night or during unseasonably cold spells until there is little risk of frosts. Keep a watch for slugs and snails as they can soon decimate seedlings if preventative measures are not taken (see p174). If growing to maturity, gradually thin out seedlings to their final spacings. Feed and water regularly.

REWARDING TOMATOES

The most popular container crop is tomatoes. These come in two main types. The first is 'indeterminate' or 'vine' tomatoes, which are upright and require staking and tying (see p150). The shoots produced in the leaf joints also need pinching out. The second type, known as 'determinate' or 'bush' tomatoes, also need support – their prolific sideshoots producing an unruly habit. Dwarf forms may also require short stakes when laden with fruit.

Plants are easily grown from seed sown indoors in spring (see p52). Alternatively, buy plug or young plants (see p80), to grow on, using peat-free,

multipurpose potting compost (see p82). Harden off plants before planting outdoors, after the risk of frost has passed, in their final pots, planters or growing bags. Also try growing methods such as ring culture (see p41).

TASTY TOMATOES

Tomatoes boast a wonderful range of shapes, colours, textures and flavours. Recent breeding has yielded compact- to dwarf-sized plants suitable for all pot sizes. With a glasshouse or conservatory you can grow all the various types. Outdoors in areas where cool, wet summers prevail, use indigenously bred cultivars and/or those with medium- to cherry-sized fruit as they yield and ripen more reliably. Also look for grafted tomatoes or those with resistance to leaf blight.

• HERBS IN POTS •

Herbs are an essential accompaniment to the kitchen, and all are ideal for growing in containers. Ideally, place them just outside the kitchen door, where they can be conveniently picked fresh for use in cooking, for infusions, as a garnish or even as potpourri.

A significant majority of herbs come from warm, sunny climates, which often experience periodic drought. To cope with this, such plants have developed a variety of common characteristics: for example, they can conserve moisture by means of their tight, shrubby habit and small, glossy or hairy leaves. They also produce essential and aromatic oils, which are exuded to help cool leaves and minimise moisture loss. The highest concentrations of oil are produced when plants are grown in strong sunlight and in not too lush conditions. This also helps ripen growth so the plants are sturdier and better able to withstand the rigours of cool-temperate winters.

A few herbs, such as lemon balm and sweet woodruff, are tolerant of cooler, shadier conditions.

SOURCING PLANTS

You can grow herbs from seed or buy plants from garden centres or specialist nurseries (see p80). The latter are a great source of plants and expertise, and many offer rareties as well as mail order and online sales. Select young plants rather than older pot-bound ones, as most herbs quickly make substantial plants.

Although all herbs can be grown from seed, some are easier and faster to grow than others. Subtropical herbs, such as basils (*Basilicum*), are generally seed raised, and because they thrive in

HERBS THAT TOLERATE SHADE

Most herbs do best in full sun and produce their strongest flavours in such sites. However, the following will tolerate shady conditions:

Chervil (*Anthriscus cerifolium*)
Chives (*Allium schoenoprasum*)
French tarragon (*Artemisia dracunculus*)
Lemon balm (*Melissa officinalis*)
Mint (*Mentha*)
Parsley (*Petroselinum crispum*)
Sweet cicely (*Myrrhis odorata*)
Sweet woodruff (*Galium odoratum*)

*Creeping, drought-tolerant thyme (*Thymus*) is both useful and decorative below this sweet bay (*Laurus nobilis*).*

warmth and humidity are better grown in the protection of a glasshouse rather than outdoors in cool-temperate areas with their variable summers.

Shrubby herbs are best grown from softwood or semiripe cuttings taken in summer, while herbaceous and bulbous herbs (such as chives) can be divided in early spring to make new plants.

HERB CARE

For most herbs use a good-quality, peat-free potting compost, with added horticultural grit or perlite to increase drainage. Place the pot in a position that gets good light for most of the day; avoid shade as plants will languish. Water the plants periodically, allowing the rootball to dry before watering again. Pinch out the tips of young plants to encourage sideshoots and a bushier habit; also the number of harvestable leaves and stems will increase. Unless specifically required, remove a good proportion of flowering shoots to maintain plant vigour. Harvest growth evenly over the whole plant.

As many herbs come from Mediterranean areas, not all are reliably hardy. Therefore, while there is a risk of frosts, protect these plants in a frost-free glasshouse or conservatory.

The leaves of chives add zest to salads, soups and stir-fries, and the edible flowers also attract pollinators such as bees.

• FRUIT IN CONTAINERS •

Many people have room to grow container-grown fruit, provided the right varieties are chosen. Besides staples such as apples, pears or strawberries you can try exciting crops such as blueberries or, given winter protection in cool-temperate climates, lemons and limes or climbing fruit such as kiwis. There are also new hybrids to try, such as those between plums and apricots (pluots and plumcots), dwarf forms of larger trees, such as quinces, and sweeter black currants and gooseberries.

TOP FRUIT

The term 'top fruit' is applied to apples, pears, cherries and quinces. These sizeable fruit trees are difficult to accommodate in pots, so select those grafted on dwarfing rootstocks to restrict their size: for example, 'M9' or 'M26' for apples; 'Quince C' for pears.

Selecting and planting

Before buying, check the fruit variety is appropriate for container cultivation (see box on p60). Also, find out if the variety is self-fertile, that is, able to set fruit by pollinating itself; this is particular important for apples, pears and cherries grown in isolation. If the

Using dwarfing rootstocks, you can enjoy your own potted orchard of fruit trees, even in restricted spaces.

variety of your choice isn't self-fertile, or is only partially so, grow another compatible cultivar alongside it, to fertilise it.

Some suppliers offer 'family trees', which are 2–3 different, but compatible, fruit varieties grafted on the same rootstock. The aim is to help pollinate cultivars not reliably self-

TOP FRUIT VARIETIES FOR CONTAINERS

Crop	Variety	Self-fertile?	Rootstock
Dessert apples	'Discovery'	No – use 'James Grieve' or 'Sunset'	'M9' or 'M26'
	'James Grieve'	Partially – use 'Discovery' or 'Sunset'	'M9' or 'M26'
	'Sunset'	No – use 'Discovery' or 'James Grieve'	'M9' or 'M26'
Pears	'Beth'	No – use 'Conference' or 'Williams' Bon Chrétien'	'Quince C'
	'Conference'	Partially – use 'Williams' Bon Chrétien' or 'Beth'	'Quince C'
	'Williams' Bon Chrétien'	Partially – use 'Conference' or 'Beth'	'Quince C'
Cherries	'Compact Stella'	Yes	'Colt' or 'Gisela 5'
	'Sunburst'	Yes	'Colt' or 'Gisela 5'
	'Van'	Yes	'Colt' or 'Gisela 5'

fertile and to produce a diverse crop of fruit from the same space.

Some trees come ready trained – as step-overs, fans and espaliers, for example. These two-dimensional trees can be very useful where space is restricted and where pots can be sited near supporting surfaces, such as walls, fences or screens.

Purchase a good-quality specimen with a straight, clear trunk topped with a few strong, evenly spaced sideshoots to form the canopy.

Trees can be purchased bare root while dormant, or ready potted. If bare root, establish the tree in a pot 3–5cm (1–2in) wider than the spread of the tree's roots. Ready potted trees may also require a larger pot to grow on. Even very dwarfed trees will eventually need a pot 38cm (15in) wide; larger trees, 60cm (24in).

Use loam-based potting compost, such as John Innes No 3 (see box on p137), rather than peat-free, multipurpose potting compost. Plant the tree at the previous soil level, with the graft point clear of the compost surface. Secure tall trees with a stake until established. Firm the compost and thoroughly water in.

Keep roots moist in warm weather, especially after fruits have set (see p142). Apply balanced general fertiliser at bud break each year, to stimulate growth (see p146). Every 3–4 years, remove each tree from its pot, scrape off some of the old compost and replenish with fresh.

Training & pruning

How a fruit tree is trained and pruned depends on its type and size. Some types of dwarf trees require very little attention, so always follow any advice that comes with them.

To develop a canopy in a young tree, remove the main shoot tip when the tree has reached the required height and shorten side branches by half to encourage sideshoots to form. These are then trained to form short, horizontal flowering spurs.

Mature trees require only trimming to shape, and pruning to create spurs. To do this simply shorten new growth by half in late summer, then prune these back further to two or three buds in winter.

Imagine the thrill of plucking a ripe tomato, strawberry or apple that you have grown on your own patio.

61

POTTED STRAWBERRIES

Fortunately, these summer favourites are easy to grow in containers. Being herbaceous perennials, they spread via runners producing rooted plantlets. Strawberries are often planted in special strawberry pots made of terracotta or plastic and with plenty of side openings through which to grow the plants (see box on p25). They are also grown in hanging baskets (see p33), growing bags (see p39) or mesh gabions (see p32).

Strawberries are divided into four main fruiting types: early, midseason, late, and ever-fruiting. Most fruit between early and late summer, while ever-fruiting cultivars produce intermittently over the season. You can grow one type or mix them to provide a continuity of fruit. Plants yield most prolifically when young, peaking at 2–3 years, so refresh with new stock every few years. Always buy from a reputable supplier, which guarantees virus-free plants, because strawberries are very susceptible to viruses, usually spread by greenfly; these cause yellowed, distorted leaves and reduced yield.

Bare-rooted plants require planting soon after receipt. Trim overlong roots and soak for 30–60 minutes before planting. Strawberries prefer light, open soil, so fill the pot with peat-free, multipurpose potting compost, rather than a loam-based one. Space plants 15–23cm (6–9in) apart. Set their crowns level with the surface, spread out the roots, cover with compost, firm and water.

When planting a strawberry pot, tuck roots into the side openings and top, filling and working compost around the roots. Line a mesh hanging basket or gabion with landscape fabric or plastic sheeting. Then slit the liner and carefully thread the plant roots through the gap, sitting the crown flush to the basket. Once plants are positioned, soak with water and allow to drain.

Strawberries crop well in pots, and you can extend the season by growing types that ripen at different times.

62

63

NUTRITIOUS BLUEBERRIES

As well as being delicious, the blueberry is also one of the so-called superfruits, that is, those high in antioxidants and other essential vitamins. Because of this, it is now a popular container plant. Highbush blueberry (*Vaccinium corymbosum*) is a twiggy, evergreen or semi-evergreen shrub, 60cm (2ft) high. It is partially self-fertile, producing clusters of round, sweet berries on short branches from early to high summer. Crops improve if different cultivars that flower together are grown close by.

Blueberries have shallow, fibrous roots and are happy in shallow urns, troughs

Blueberries are suitable for container growing as containers allow you to provide the damp, acid soil they need.

or raised planters. They prefer dappled shade to direct sun, so are ideal for easterly or northerly sites. Keep roots cool and moist and avoid them drying out in hot sun, which may cause damage.

Plants require moist, acid conditions to thrive, so always use ericaceous potting compost – failure to provide suitable conditions results in yellow leaves, stunted growth and poor harvests. Remove dead leaves and prune weak shoots; repot every few years (see p148).

ORNAMENTAL
PLANTS IN
CONTAINERS

• POPULAR ORNAMENTAL PLANTS •

Whatever style statement you yearn to create with your container plantings there are legions of beautiful and distinctive ornamental plants to help realise your ideas. Some really stand out (see pp67–79) and have become the backbone of many container displays. If their basic needs are met, and they are given a little space, regular water and liquid feed they will flower prolifically over many months.

PLANT TYPES

The majority of successful container plants are hardy and/or tender annuals (see pp95 and 124) and perennials (see pp92 and 130), but shrubs (see pp89 and

132), bulbs (see pp83 and 126) and the more vigorous alpines (see p105) are also popular choices.

If you are intending to have a mixed planting in a large container, plan the effects before sowing, purchasing or planting. You need demure, quiet plants to counterbalance those that scream. Placing too many colourful, high-impact plants together is likely to result in a chaotic effect, so introduce such plants sparingly, placing them where they will make the right kind of display.

Drought-tolerant, long-flowering pelargoniums, some with variegated foliage, are useful in a potted collection.

• PLANTS ON OFFER •

The following is a selection of high-calibre container plants that will stimulate your planting palette.

Abutilon (Flowering maple) Tender to hardy shrubs, 60cm–1.2m (2–4ft), with maple-like leaves, often variegated. Pendent, bell-like flowers in yellow, orange, red and pink. Full sun, with some moisture.

Agastache (Giant hyssop) Tender to hardy, aromatic perennials from Mexico in the mint family. Thin, tubular flowers in shades of yellow, orange and white on spikes 30–60cm (1–2ft) long in summer. Full sun. Drought-tolerant.

Ageratum (Floss flower) Tender annuals or perennials, 15–20cm (6–8in) tall, from tropical America. Heads of fluffy flowers in blue, pink and white. Sun, with some moisture. Good massed with other plants.

Angelonia angustifolia (Summer snapdragon) Tender, tufted, evergreen

Flowering maples are long-flowered shrubs useful as single features or massed with other seasonal bedding.

perennials, 20–30cm (8–12in) tall, from Mexico. Spikes of squat, snapdragon-like flowers in pink, purple, blue or white in midsummer.

Antirrhinum (Snapdragon) Hardy annuals, 15–30cm (6–12in) tall, with upright stems. Spikes of narrow, pouched flowers in all colours, except blue. Good for massing or supporting other plants.

Argyranthemum Tender, shrubby plants, 30–45cm (12–18in) tall, in the daisy family from the Canary Isles. Flowers in red, pink, yellow, sunset shades and white, often with attractive, finely dissected foliage.

Arctotis (African daisy) Tender, silver-leaved perennials, 15cm (6in) tall, from South Africa. Flowers in sultry shades of red, orange and yellow. Drought-tolerant. Flowers open in full sun.

Aurinia syn. *Alyssum* Spring-flowering, evergreen perennials, 10–30cm (4–12in) tall. Enduring flowers in dense heads of yellow, cream and white. Good with late spring bulbs or edging containers.

Begonia Diverse group of tender plants invaluable for both flowers and foliage. Annual *B. semperflorens* is tufted with rounded, fleshy leaves and clusters of small flowers in red, pink and white.

Arching bedding begonias bred from scarlet B. boliviensis are shade-tolerant and excellent for pots, baskets or pouches.

Cascading hybrids of *B. boliviensis* with flowers in red, orange and white are good for pots and baskets, as are tuberous begonias with their large flowers, 10–15cm (4–6in) across.

Bidens Climbing plants with lax stems and ferny foliage. Yellow, daisy-like flowers all summer until frosts. Useful as gap filler or basket plant or for edging.

Brachyscome iberidifolia (Swan river daisy) Tufted annuals, to 45cm (18in) tall, from Australia. Produces filigree foliage and small, daisy-like flowers in blue, purple, pink or white from late summer to first frosts.

Brugmansia (Angels' trumpet) Stout, tender shrubs, to 1.8m (6ft) or more tall, from the Americas, with large leaves. Large, pendent flowers, single or double, in red, pink, orange, cream and white. Prefers sun, shelter and moist conditions.

Calceolaria (Slipper flower) Annuals or tender perennials, 15–30cm (6–12in) tall, grown for their distinctive, pouched or flared flowers in red, yellow or orange. Prefer sun, shelter and moisture. Feature plant.

Calibrachoa see *Petunia*.

Callistephus (China aster) Hardy annuals, 20–60cm (8–24in) tall, from China. Single or double, fringed, daisy-like flowers in blue, lilac, pink, red or white. Long-flowered; good for cutting.

Canna (Canna lily, Indian shot plant) Tender, subtropical, rhizomatous perennials, 0.6m–1.8m (2–6ft) tall. Broad leaves can be bronzed or

Angels' trumpet is a spectacular shrub for a sunny, sheltered spot, revelling when kept moist and well fed.

The vibrant flowers and sumptuous, often purple-tinted leaves of Indian shot plant make a visually arresting sight.

variegated. Flamboyant flowers in all shades, except blue, all summer.

Celosia (Cockscomb, Feather plant) Tender annuals, 25–30cm (10–12in) tall, with brightly coloured, feathery flowers in pink, red, yellow and orange. Prefers sun, shelter and some moisture.

Clarkia syn. Godetia Annuals, 30–60cm (1–2ft) or more tall, from California. Flowers cup-shaped, in shades of red, pink and lilac, often blotched. Good for massing or growing with others. Full sun.

Cosmos Tender annuals or perennials, 0.6–1.8m (2–6ft) tall, from central America, with filigree foliage. Long-lasting, daisy-like flowers from summer to autumn. *C. bipinnatus* has single, double or quilled flowers in red, white or pink; *C. sulphureus* in yellow or orange. Full sun, with moisture.

Dahlia Tender, vigorous, tuberous perennials, 0.6–1.8m (2–6ft) tall, from South America. Many cultivars, with flowers in many shapes, single and double, and in all colours and combinations, except blue. New compact cultivars have dark foliage.

Dianthus (Pink) Tufted or mat-like annuals or perennials, 10–30cm (4–12in), with green or blue needle foliage. Flowers erect, with fringed petals generally red, pink or white. Often sweetly perfumed. Useful in baskets or for edging pots.

Diascia (Twin flower) Mat-forming annuals or perennials, 10–20cm (4–8in) tall, from South Africa. Squat-foxglove flowers all summer in shades of red, coral, pink and mauve. Prefers sun, with some moisture.

Dichondra micrantha 'Silver Falls' Prostrate creepers grown for their intensely silvery, kidney-shaped foliage. Ideal for pot edges and hanging baskets, where shoots fall to 1m (3ft) or more. Full sun. Drought-tolerant.

Drosanthemum Hardy, evergreen succulents, to 15cm (6in) tall, forming a spreading mat. Studded with small, daisy-like flowers all summer. Full sun. Drought-tolerant. Good for baskets. Avoid shade from other plants.

Whole ranges of dahlias are being specifically bred for pots, such as pink-striped, dark-leaved D. 'Mystic Dreamer'.

70

Erysimum (Wallflower) Spring-flowering, hardy, shrubby, evergreen perennials, 30–60cm (1–2ft) tall. Heads of cabbage-like flowers in red, orange, yellow, purple and pink. Sun to semishade. Excellent with bulbs.

Eschscholtzia (Californian poppy) Tufted annuals, 15–30cm (6–12in) tall, with blue-green, filigree leaves. Short-lived, poppy-like flowers in many colours, except blue, over a long season. Full sun. Drought-tolerant.

Felicia amelloides (Blue daisy) Tender, small-leaved, evergreen perennials, 20–30cm (8–12in) tall, from South Africa. Produces blue daisies all summer. Prefers sun. Drought-tolerant.

Fuchsia Tender to hardy shrubs, 0.6–1m (1–3ft) or more tall, grown for their pendent, ballerina-like flowers borne throughout summer and autumn. Flowers single and double in red, pink, mauve and lilac combinations. Erect and pendent forms make ideal focal points for pots and hanging baskets.

Gaura (Bee blossom) Tender, upright, evergreen perennials, 38–120cm (15–48in) tall, from south USA, with

Fuchsias are versatile shrubs with upright, spreading or weeping habits and can be trained into a standard, as here.

thin stems. White to pink, airy flowers produced all summer. Ideal when threaded through taller plants.

Gazania Tender perennials, 15–23cm (6–9in) tall, from South Africa with evergreen rosettes. Brightly coloured, multitoned flowers in yellow, orange, red, pink and brown appear all summer. Needs sun and well-drained conditions.

Gerbera Tender to relatively hardy, evergreen perennials, 60–1m (2–3ft) tall, from South Africa. Single or double, daisy-like flowers in range of bright colours, except blue. Prefers shelter and warmth.

***Glechoma hederacea* 'Variegata'** (Variegated ground ivy) Prostrate, groundcover perennials grown for their softly variegated, toothed leaves. Good for baskets and pot edges. Shade- and drought-tolerant.

Hedera (Ivy) Prostrate or climbing, evergreen ground cover grown for their wide range of leaf shapes and variegation. Ideal for hanging baskets and pot edges. Very shade- and drought-tolerant.

Hedychium (Ginger lily) Tender, rhizomatous perennials on cane-like stems, 1–1.8m (3–6ft) thick, with narrow leaves.

Indispensable for sun or shade, drought or wet, ivies are usually used as edging plants, but can be trained into topiary shapes.

Torch-like flower spikes in yellow, orange and white are borne from late summer to first frosts.

Helichrysum Shrubby perennials with arching stems, used for their grey-felted leaves. *H. petiolare*, 1m (3ft) tall, is available in variegated and yellow-leaved forms; *H. microphyllum* is smaller and more silvery.

Heliotropium (Cherry pie, heliotrope) Shrubby, evergreen perennials, 30cm

73

Evergreen, shade-tolerant Heuchera (Coral flower) are available in a wide range of colours and patterns.

(12in) tall, with textured leaves and small, fragrant flowerheads in blue, purple, pink and white. Attractive to butterflies and moths. Ideal for pot edges and hanging baskets.

Heuchera (Coral flower) and **x Heucherella** Clump-forming, durable, evergreen perennials, 15–30cm (6–12in) tall, with coloured and patterned leaves. Fine wands of flowers in summer. Highly shade-tolerant. Striking foliage plants.

Isotoma axillaris (Rock isotome) Tender, busy, herbaceous perennials, 15–30cm (6–12in) tall, from Australia, grown for their blue to mauve flowers. Ideal as an edging plant or mixed with other ornamentals.

Lathyrus odoratus (Sweet pea) Annual climbers, to 3.7m (12ft) tall. Elegant, pea-like flowers in most shades, except bright yellow. Many cultivars are sweet scented and make excellent cut flowers. Most cultivars need support.

Lavatera (Mallow) Annuals or tender to hardy, shrubby perennials, 1–1.8m (3–6ft) tall. Bold, circular flowers in pink and white, often blotched red. Long-flowered, from early summer to autumn. Sun, drought-tolerant.

Lobelia Slender-shooted perennials, 15cm (6in) tall, grown as annuals. A mass of small, lobed flowers from spring to autumn in blue, pink, purple, red and white. Ideal for baskets and containers.

Lobularia (Sweet alyssum) Tufted annuals, 10–20cm (4–8in) tall, with fragrant flowerheads early spring into summer, usually white but also pink and purple. Good with bulbs. Partial shade.

Mesembryanthemum crystallinum
(Ice plant) Prostrate, tender perennials, grown as annuals, 10cm (4in) tall, from South Africa, with fleshy leaves covered in clear 'beads'. Daisy-like flowers in iridescent colours of red, pink, yellow, orange and white, open in full sun.

Mimulus (Monkey flower, musk) Hardy and tender perennials or annuals, 10–30cm (4–12in) tall, grown for their cheerful flowers in shades of red, yellow and orange. Grow in sun or partial shade, but keep moist.

Myosotis (Forget-me-not) Tufted, spring-flowering perennials or annuals, 10–20cm (4–8in) tall, producing clusters of small, circular, lobed flowers in blue, pink and white. A good partner for bulbs.

Nemesia Tender annuals, perennials or subshrubs, 15–60cm (6–24in) tall, from South Africa. Small, snapdragon-like flowers in vibrant shades of red, orange, yellow and blue.

Nicotiana (Tobacco plant) Annuals or tender perennials producing spikes clothed in slender, tubed flowers in muted colours, fragrant at night. Dwarf cultivars, 30cm

Annual or shrubby mallows bear satin-sheened, pink or white flowers over a long period.

(12in) tall, are used for bedding, while taller varieties make good feature plants.

Osteospermum Tender, shrubby perennials from South Africa, producing pastel, daisy-like flowers throughout summer. Some are prostrate; others 30–60cm (1–2ft) tall, clothed in neat, midgreen leaves.

Pelargonium (Geranium) Diverse plants, 15–60cm (6–24in) tall, from South Africa. The zonal pelargonium *P. × hortorum* has rounded leaves with a central blotch, and flowers in shades of red, pink, salmon and white. The ivy-leaved pelargonium *P. peltatum* has lax growth and looser heads of flowers, ideal for edging hanging baskets and containers.

Penstemon (Beard tongue) Hardy to tender herbaceous perennials, 0.6–1m (1–3ft) tall, from the USA, with tubular flowers in a wide range of colours, often with contrasting throat. Long-flowered.

Petunia Upright or trailing annuals or short-lived perennials, 15–30cm (6–12in) tall, with flared flowers in primary and muted colours, often blotched or multitoned. Related but smaller, shrubbier **Calibrachoa** has small, bell-like, multicoloured flowers. Good for edging.

Portulaca (Rose moss) Tender perennials, 10–15cm (4–6in) tall, with low, branching habit and fleshy, succulent leaves. Small, cupped flowers in all shades except blue. Full sun. Keep well drained. Drought-tolerant.

Primula (Primrose and polyanthus) Hardy, spring-flowering herbaceous perennials, 10–30cm (4–12in) tall, with

LEFT *Petunias and pansies are the floral cornerstones of container planting, with pansy cultivars available all year round.*

OPPOSITE *Cascading ivy-leaved pelargoniums are ideal edging plants, such as here with petunias and nemesia.*

leafy rosettes. Primrose flowers are on single stalks, while those of polyanthus cluster on a stout stem. Needs cool, moist conditions. Good massed with bulbs.

Rhodochiton (Purple bell vine) Tender, twining perennial vines from Mexico, with unusual, hanging, dark purple, tubular flowers and maroon calyces. Good in baskets or cascading over pots.

Salvia (Sage) Branching, tender perennials largely grown for their striking summer flowers. *S. coccinea* (Texas sage), 0.6–1m (2–3ft) tall, scarlet flowers; *S. splendens* (scarlet sage), 15–30cm (6–12in) tall, has spikes in red, pink, white, salmon and dark purple.

Sanvitalia procumbens (Creeping zinnia) Prostrate annuals from Mexico. Small, black-centred flowers in yellow or orange. Best in sun or semishade.

Scaevola aemula (Fairy fan-flower) Spreading evergreen perennials, 15–25cm (6–10in) tall, from Australia. Lobed flowers in blue, pink or white in summer. Sun or semishade. Good as edging.

Schizanthus (Butterfly flower, poor man's orchid) Tender annuals or biennials, 15–30cm (6–12in) tall, from Chile, with dissected foliage. Flowers in exhilarating colours in summer. Needs warmth and moisture.

Senecio cineraria Evergreen subshrubs, 30–60cm (1–2ft) tall, from the Mediterranean, with dissected, silvery foliage. Often grown as an annual. Drought-tolerant. Ideal for contrasting with other ornamentals.

Solenostemon (Coleus) Tender shrubby perennials, 0.3–1m (1–3ft) tall, grown for their brightly coloured, patterned leaves. Pinch out flowers as they form. Good focal plant.

Sutera syn. ***Bacopa*** Tender, creeping perennials, 10–15cm (4–6in) tall, from South Africa with small leaves and tiny, lobed flowers in lilac, pink, blue and white. Excellent for baskets and edging.

Tagetes patula (French marigold) and ***T. erecta*** (African marigold). Tufted annuals, 10–30cm (4–12in) tall, from the Americas. Dense flowers in yellow, orange or maroon. Aromatic foliage.

Thunbergia alata (Black-eyed Susan) Tender, twining perennials, 0.6m–1.8m

(2–6ft), from east Africa. Dark-eyed flowers in yellow, cream, orange and red. Sun or semishade. Needs support.

Torenia (Wishbone flower) Tender annuals, 30–45cm (12–18in) tall, from Vietnam, with blotched, tubular flowers in blue, pink and yellow. Prefers semishade, warmth and moisture.

Verbena Spreading, evergreen subshrubs, 10–15cm (4–6in) tall , with toothed leaves and heads of star-shaped flowers in a range of vibrant and subtle tones. Good for edging.

Viola including **V. × wittrockiana** (Pansy) Annuals or short-lived perennials, 10–20cm (4–8in) tall, with oval flowers in all colours, often

Peacocks of the annual world, zinnias revel in full sun, producing long-lasting flowers on bushy, upright plants.

patterned or with 'faces'. Long-flowered. Available all year round. Performs best in semishade. Needs moisture.

Xeranthemum (Everlasting flower) Erect annuals, 15–45cm (6–18in) tall, with long-lasting, papery, daisy-like flowers in cream, yellow, red, orange, pink and red. Good as cut flowers. Drought-tolerant.

Zinnia Long-flowering, drought-tolerant annuals, 0.6–1m (1–3ft) tall, from Mexico. Flowers, either single or double, in all colours, except blue. Full sun. Single flowers good for butterflies.

• PURCHASING PLANTS •

Bedding plants are available in their appropriate seasons from local sources such as garden or DIY centres, nurseries and market stalls (see box below). However, these may not offer everything you need for your container plantings.

For a more extensive range, source your plants from mail order retailers (see p81). Alternatively, if you have a conservatory, glasshouse or cold frame, why not grow your own plants from seed (see p124)? As well as having an even wider choice than bought plants, you also obtain more plants for a lower outlay and enjoy the satisfaction of growing your own plants to maturity.

PREMATURE PURCHASES

Choose plants that are fresh, clean and healthy, well rooted and with plenty of new shoots or flower buds. Avoid those that are wilted (see p177), have yellowing leaves or look spent.

Beware of purchasing half-hardy or tender bedding plants too early in spring if you can't protect them in a conservatory, glasshouse or cold frame. With frosts or cold nights still possible until early summer in some areas, such young plants can become cold-checked or killed if they have not been hardened off by suppliers before being offered for sale. Planting out vulnerable tender

BUYING LOCALLY

Local outlets often provide the most reliable source of plants and you can buy with confidence. You can see what you're getting, better judge the quality of the plants and obtain plants in various sizes from specimens down to plug sizes. In cases of complaint, you can often return the plants for a refund or exchange. It's a good idea to try things out by placing the pot and plants together to see how they look and how many are needed before purchasing them.

Purchasing by mail order is a popular way of obtaining plants. Open packaging and pot up plants as soon as possible.

plants before the frosts have finished is likely to result in casualties.

BUYING BY MAIL ORDER

This is a convenient way of obtaining plants, particularly if you are nervous about raising from seed, or don't have the time or facilities to do so. Plants are usually purchased as seed or cuttings-raised plantlets, ready for you to grow on. You can also buy specimen-sized plants, but with the attendant increase in the cost of plants and postage.

Suppliers offer an ever-increasing range of plant types and cultivars, which are sold via catalogues, flyers, advertisements or on the internet. Companies vary from substantial nurseries and national retailers to individuals – the last are particularly prevalent on online auction sites.

Cheap offers abound, but wherever possible purchase from a reputable source with a history of supplying by mail order and which guarantees high-quality stock. Such a supplier should have the requisite packaging experience to ensure safe transit for your plants via

the post or a courier. It is also helpful if the supplier specifies and illustrates the size of plants available.

New arrivals by mail order

On receipt of your mail-order plants, remove the outer cardboard packaging, thereby exposing the plants to light. Plug plants are usually inserted in a moulded, inner, plastic sleeve. Crack this open and pot up the plants. If you are unable to plant them immediately, water the plugs and place the opened package in a warm but shady site. Take off any polythene wrapping from larger, ready-potted plants, remove any debris and

Ensure plants are moist before planting, firm compost around the rootball and water the container thoroughly.

water. Trees, shrubs, and fruit trees are purchased potted or bare root. If potted, water compost if dry. Bare root plants are mailed when dormant. Moisten roots and either pot up immediately or dig a hole and cover roots with soil until required.

POTTING OFF

Plant each plug plant into a pot 5–7.5cm (2–3in) wider than its soil plug, using a good-quality, peat-free potting compost. Water plants in and label each, especially if you have ordered different cultivars of the same type of plant, such as fuchsia or petunia. Place the pots in warm conditions and in good light, but avoid strong sunlight for a few days until plants become accustomed to their new conditions. In hot weather, place the plants beneath the glasshouse staging or under a screen of horticultural fleece.

Check them regularly for signs of establishment, such as roots poking from the bottom of the pot. Then pot them on into larger containers, and feed with a balanced liquid feed each week. Pinch out the growth tips to encourage sideshoots to form, resulting in a bushier plant, more shoots and the potential for more flowers. Once there is little risk of frost, harden off plants (see p125) and put outdoors in their final pots.

• BULBS & CORMS
IN CONTAINERS •

Bulbs are the quintessential spring flowers, and ideal for a bright and breezy blast of colour to dispel winter blues. Within 'bulbs' are included any plant possessing a swollen underground organ containing food reserves: for example, crocus and montbretia (*Crocosmia*) store their food in corms; iris have rhizomes; and dahlia use tubers.

All are well suited to container growing because they are compact, almost guaranteed to perform and can be densely planted to maximise the number of flowers from a given space. However, while spring might be considered their main season, there are beautiful bulbs that perform throughout summer and into late autumn.

BULB POTENTIAL
Bulbous plants can be used in so many exciting ways. Mass a single species or

LAYER PLANTING

Bulbs planted to flower after each other are one of the joys of container gardening. The wider the container, the more bulbs you can pack in, but you need to moderate the complexity of the display to fit the container diameter, and allow sufficient depth for the largest bulbs (see box on p129) as well as a 2–2.5cm (³/₄–1in) gap for watering. Fill the container with growing medium at a height suitable for the largest bulbs. Starting with the largest at the centre, work out to the pot edge. Add more compost and plant smaller bulbs into the remaining gaps at their required height. Lightly firm and give a thorough soak with water.

BULBS & CORMS FOR A PURPOSE

Winter & spring	Summer	Autumn	
Crocus	Allium	Amaryllis	Nerine bowdenii
Galanthus	(ornamental	belladonna	and cvs
(snowdrop)	onion)	(belladonna lily)	Schizostylis coccinea
Hyacinthus	Begonia	Colchicum (autumn	(kaffir lily) and
(hyacinth)	Dahlia	crocus) (many	cvs
Narcissus	Eucomis	spp. and cvs)	Scilla autumnalis
(daffodil)	(pineapple lily)	Crocus (autumn-	Sternbergia lutea
Muscari (grape	Ixia (corn lily)	flowering spp.	(autumn
hyacinth)	Lilium (lily)	e.g. C. speciosus)	daffodil)
Scilla	Tigridia (tiger	Cyclamen	Zephranthes
Tulipa (tulip)	flower)	hederifolium	candida
			(windflower)

cultivar together for a bold statement or vividly contrast different cultivars of the same type of bulb together. Try mixing different types of bulb flowering at the same time or with careful selection use bulbs flowering at slightly different times to provide a succession of bloom (see box on p83).

Bulbs are also useful gap fillers for beds and borders, providing continuity for lulls in the display, the pots either placed in the vacant space or dug into the ground. For optimum results, always choose best-quality bulbs (see p127).

Bulbs, such as daffodils (*Narcissus*), hyacinths (*Hyacinthus*) and amaryllis (*Hippeastrum*), can be forced to flower earlier than usual indoors if special, heat-treated bulbs are used. Being grown intensively is not ideal long term, so when the display is over the pot can be dismantled and the bulbs discarded or planted out in the garden, but they may take time to flower prolifically again.

BULB GROWING CONDITIONS

Bulbs need well-drained potting compost, particularly if they are to be grown intensively; it doesn't need to be rich in nutrients. Use a good-quality, peat-free growing medium, adding additional grit or perlite for drainage. Orientate the bulbs correctly, and plant at the correct depth (see box on p129).

Unless planting with other ornamentals, most bulbs do not require deep containers – one wider than high is ideal for potted bulb displays. You do, however, need to ensure there is sufficient depth of compost for the developing roots to anchor and support the top growth of the bulb. Large tuberous plants, such as dahlia and taro (*Colocasia*), produce roots below the shoot but above the storage organ, so ensure there are a few centimetres of potting compost above the tuber to enable their establishment.

General bulb care involves removing spent flowerheads and keeping plants watered (see p129). After flowering, bulbs benefit from an occasional liquid feed using a balanced fertiliser (see p146). Some summer bulbs, such as begonia, Indian shot plant (*Canna*) and dahlia, are not frost hardy.

Bulbs can be relied on for floral impact, whether used en masse or as incidental elements in mixed plantings.

In autumn, remove spent compost and overwinter in a frost-free location before starting them off again in spring.

If bulbs are planted among other ornamentals, it is often more practical to remove them after flowering, use the space for bedding and replace with new bulbs the following season.

BULB LONGEVITY
While most will thrive long-term given a little care, some bulbs, such as large hybrid tulips, may not persist for more than a year or two and are best replaced each year using new stock.

• HARDY TREES IN CONTAINERS •

Trees make the biggest statement in a garden and can do so in a container, too, as long as each has a big enough pot to accommodate it and its needs are met. Containerised trees can be a useful solution for courtyard gardens, which have no soil, or in situations where you need to frame a view or doorway, mark a boundary, accentuate an aspect of a design or partially screen an eyesore.

Growing trees in containers will, however, severely restrict their size and and they will never reach their mature proportions. Some can be lightly pruned to improve bushiness of the canopy or be more heavily trained and shaped at topiary to create standard mopheads and other geometric shapes (see p160).

TREE CHOICES

Trees that have some degree of drought-tolerance and fibrous root systems are better for pot culture than those with sparse, fleshy roots or taproots. Columnar or fastigiated forms are good as sentinels, where a vertical accent is required or where space is restricted.

Evergreen trees, such as holly (*Ilex*), sweet bay (*Laurus nobilis*), yew (*Taxus*) and cherry laurel (*Prunus laurocerasus*) are all drought- and shade-tolerant, and will create year-round impact, especially in winter; they can also be pruned into a variety of shapes. Holly has a range of beautiful, variegated forms, and if self-fertile (or female and pollinated) will produce bright displays of berries, further enhancing the decorative effects.

Deciduous trees can reveal interesting branch shapes and colours in winter, and some, such as hornbeam (*Carpinus*) and beech (*Fagus*), will retain their dried, burnished leaves of the previous year to provide further winter interest.

Not all trees are appropriate for growing in containers, however,

TREES THAT CAN BE GROWN IN CONTAINERS

Acer (maple)
Betula (birch)
Buxus sempervirens (common box)
Carpinus betulus (common hornbeam)
Fagus sylvatica (common beech)
Ilex (holly)
Laurus nobilis (sweet bay)
Pinus (pine)
Prunus laurocerasus (cherry laurel)
Taxus baccata (yew)

and in some circumstances a large, multistemmed shrub may offer a better planting solution than a tree.

TREE CARE

For most trees, loam-based John Innes No 3 potting compost is ideal (see box on p137). If growing lime-intolerant types, such as rhododendron or magnolia, then use potting compost especially formulated for such ericaceous plants.

To keep them growing strongly and healthily, trees require as much care and attention as any other potted plant (see pp142–161). Neglect not only results in damaging the plant, but also in a tree that becomes an eyesore.

Ideally, large specimen trees should be grown in durable polypropylene containers, because terracotta and other fragile materials can be damaged when manhandled in the potting process and if blown over by strong wind. Pots made of such materials are also costly to replace. Roots adhere to the sides of terracotta pots, making it difficult to extract the rootball when potting on, which is needed every few years to help maintain the health and vitality of the tree (see p132).

Eventually, it becomes unfeasible to keep increasing the pot size for a tree,

87

Site trees in pots carefully out of strong winds, which may scorch foliage or topple them, damaging both pot and plant.

even though its root system fills the current container. Instead, you should replenish the potting compost. This can be tackled in two ways.

The simplest is to scrape off 3–5cm (1–2in) of old compost from the surface of the rootball with a hand cultivator and replace this with fresh potting compost of the same type as previously. This can be done annually or every other year, and it provides a small area for

88

Keep woody plants watered in prolonged hot conditions as foliage can die back or fall if the rootball dries out completely.

roots to colonise and obtain nutrients. The second, more strenuous way to replenish the potting compost requires two people. It may also involve transferring the container to a more convenient site (see p156).

When in an appropriate place, remove any weeds and other detritus, then loosen the rootball from the pot by rocking the tree from side to side. Place the pot and tree on its side, and with one hand holding the pot rim and the other the tree trunk gently ease out the rootball. Rotate the pot, knocking the side to help dislodge the rootball. Once extracted, stand the tree upright.

With a hand cultivator or fork, work the tines among the roots at the side of the rootball, dislodging at least 2.5cm (¾in) depth of old compost. Tease out the matted bundles of roots, taking care to avoid damaging any main roots. Snip off any that are damaged or dead. Repeat the process beneath and on the surface of the rootball. Check for signs of disease or pests (see p170) and take appropriate action to control them.

Scrub the pot thoroughly, again looking for pests and treat as necessary. Ensure you clear away any residue soil mark near the container rim and that the drainage holes are clear (see p140). Fill the bottom of the pot with drainage material, then fresh potting compost. Ensure the amount of compost added raises the rootball to provide a 5cm (2in) depth below the rim of the pot, to allow for watering. Take care to measure this, to minimise having to lift the tree with its heavy rootball. Once positioned carefully work in fresh compost down the sides and firm to remove air pockets. Water in thoroughly and repeat a few days later.

• HARDY SHRUBS IN CONTAINERS •

Almost all shrubs can be grown in containers, offering a range of exciting planting solutions that thrive in full sun to dense shade. Combine this with a great variety of shapes, textures and colours, and seasonal highlights, such as scented flowers or autumn colour, and you can see why shrubs are indispensable.

NEW OPPORTUNITIES

Growing shrubs in containers also has practical benefits. You can create plant-specific conditions for certain shrubs that may not be suitable for the soil or climate in your garden. Other shrubs,

such as viburnum and cotoneaster, can be creatively pruned (see p91) to reveal their intricate branch structure. Japanese maples – mostly cultivars of *Acer palmatum* – are ideal for sheltered, cool, semishaded conditions, their elegant habit and soft, delicate foliage creating a refined, elegant focal point.

For a bold, architectural statement, use mahonia with its distinctive ruffs of spiky, evergreen leaves and wands

Architectural evergreens, such as box, yew or other conifers, can be used to punctuate a design or frame an entrance.

89

SHRUBS WITH A PURPOSE

Permanent shade

Aucuba japonica (spotted laurel) and
  variegated cvs
Camellia japonica cvs, *C.* x *williamsii* cvs
Fatsia japonica (Japanese aralia)
Rhododendron (many spp. and hybrids)
Sarcococca confusa (sweet box)

Full sun

Caryopteris x *clandonensis* (all cvs)
Cotinus coggygria (smoke bush) (all cvs)
Juniperus chinensis (Chinese juniper)
  (all cvs)
Santolina (all spp. and cvs)
Yucca (all spp. and cvs)

Cold, windy locations

Cornus alba (red-barked dogwood)
Euonymus fortunei (spindle tree) and cvs
Hydrangea paniculata 'Grandiflora'
Mahonia aquifolium (oregon grape)
Rhododendron yakushimanum

Scent in winter and early spring

Coronilla valentina subsp. *glauca*
Daphne bholua cvs
Hamamellis x *intermedia* 'Arnold Promise'
  (witch hazel) and other cvs
Mahonia x *media* cvs
Sarcococca (sweet box) (all species)
Viburnum x *bodnantense*

of bright yellow, scented flowers in spring, or try evergreen Japanese aralia (*Fatsia japonica*), with its bold, fan-like leaves. Hardy palms, such as Chusan palms (*Trachycarpus fortunei* or *T. wagnerianus*), lend an air of year-round, subtropical exuberance; they are excellent in half-barrels or large tubs. Black bamboo (*Phyllostachys nigra*) or golden bamboo (*P. aurea*) look chic in pots, particularly if old canes are removed to create a see-through effect. A potted shrub can also be used as the visual anchor for a group of pots.

FRAGRANT REWARDS

Scent is an important part of the garden experience, and many shrubs possess seductive and enticing aromas. There is a scented shrub in flower every day of the year, particularly in winter and spring, so with careful choice you can always have perfumed plants.

UNDERPLANTING SHRUBS

In larger containers it may be possible to underplant shrubs with tough, shade- or drought-tolerant groundcover plants, such as coral flowers (*Heuchera*),

× *Heucherella,* lesser periwinkle (*Vinca minor*), ivies (*Hedera*) or tussocky grasses and sedges (*Carex*). Bear in mind that the ground cover will compete with the shrub for resources, so ensure they are kept adequately fed and watered when in growth (see pp142, 146).

SAFE LOCATION

As with trees, shrubs need siting with care, selecting the right plant for the right place. In cool-temperate areas in winter, move potted evergreens to a sheltered position or cover with hessian sheeting (see p152). Never locate potted shrubs where water collects in winter, as prolonged waterlogging can kill them (see box on p140). Move or raise pots off the ground to aid drainage.

ARTISTIC PRUNING

Almost all shrubs need pruning for artistic and/or practical reasons. Artistically, this involves controlling the shape of the plant, revealing branch structure or creating topiary. Shrubs such as dogwoods (*Cornus*) are often grown for the colour of their bare stems

Small-leaved, evergreen shrubs, such as box, can be pruned into shapes or trained on a framework to create figures.

in winter, most vividly produced on young shoots. These are encouraged by cutting back ('coppicing') stems to 30cm (1ft) every 2–3 years, or by removing a selection of shoots annually.

PRACTICAL PRUNING

Shrubs are pruned to maintain health or enhance flowering (see p160). Thin out congested growth and remove crossing shoots to improve air flow and prevent fungal diseases (see p170). Heavy pruning of the main branch structure will prevent flowering for a year or possibly more.

91

• HARDY PERENNIALS
IN CONTAINERS •

Almost all hardy perennial plants can be used to create sumptuous, seasonal displays in pots and containers. The trick is to know which to select and how to mix them together to create the best effects. The wonderful advantage of perennials is that they provide seasonal floral highlights all year round, and many produce leaves in all manner of shapes, colours and textures to add further, longer-term interest to the display when the flowers have gone.

PERENNIAL POTENTIAL

Evergreen perennials are often used as groundcover plants, and they provide interest throughout the year. Many perennials are also fairly quick growing, and if planted with others will create a tapestry of foliage and flower. Large, deciduous perennials take time to reach their annual maximum, and there are few that have a tightly constrained growth habit.

All perennials are good at creating an air of unfettered exuberance, particularly if using bold perennials, such as cardoons (*Cynara cardunculus*) or grasses such as miscanthus. Even when spent, the foliage held on stout stems of many larger perennials will often colour richly in autumn, before drying to burnished tones for winter.

Many perennials have persistent seedheads, too, and when these become frosted the fleeting effects they produce can be breathtaking. The many cultivars of grasses, such as miscanthus and purple

Pots of hardy perennials offer many exciting ways to arrange flowers and foliage that highlight the seasons.

92

PERENNIALS WITH A PURPOSE

Feature perennials
Acanthus mollis (bear's breeches)
Agapanthus (African lily)
Angelica gigas
Cynara cardunculus (cardoon)
Grasses, such as *Arundo donax* (giant
    reed), *Miscanthus sinensis* and *Stipa
    gigantea* (giant feather grass)
Hosta (plantain lily) (large leaved)
Kniphofia (red hot poker)
Ligularia dentata (golden groundsel)
Thalictrum delavayi (meadow rue)

Long-flowering perennials
Achillea (yarrow)
Anthemis tinctoria (golden marguerite)
Coreopsis (tickseed)
Gaillardia (blanket flower)
Geranium (cranesbill)
Hemerocallis (daylily)
Penstemon
Salvia nemorosa (sage)

Perennials for foliage
Acanthus (bear's breeches)
Bergenia (elephant's ears)
Epimedium (barrenwort)
Euphorbia (spurge)
Grasses such as *Elymus* (wild rye),
    Hakonechloa, Helictotrichon and
    Miscanthus
Heuchera (coral flower) and x *Heucherella*
Hosta (plantain lily)
Phlomis

Sedum spectabile (ice plant)
Verbascum (mullein)

Perennials for edging
Alchemilla (lady's mantle)
Cerastium tomentosum (snow in summer)
Dianthus (pink)
Geranium (cranesbill)
Heuchera (coral flower) and x *Heucherella*
Origanum (marjoram)
Stachys byzantina (lamb's ears)
Veronica (speedwell)

Perennials for full sun
Agapanthus (African lily)
Anthemis
Dianthus (pink)
Euphorbia (spurge)
Geranium (cranesbill)
Grasses, such as *Festuca* (fescue),
    Helictotrichon and *Pennisetum*
Penstemon
Potentilla (cinquefoil)
Sedum (stonecrop)

Perennials for shade
Alchemilla mollis (lady's mantle)
Bergenia (elephant's ears)
Convallaria (lily-of-the-valley)
Epimedium (barrenwort)
Ferns, such as *Dryopteris* (buckler fern)
    and *Polystichum* (shield fern)
Helleborus (hellebore)
Lirope (lilyturf)

Perennials can be vulnerable to wind damage, so tie tall stems to bamboo canes using unobtrusive, green twine.

moor grass (*Molinia*), are particularly effective – their leaves rustling in the wind; cut off their stems in late winter to make way for new growth.

PLANNING PERENNIALS

It helps to marshal your thoughts into which plants to choose, particularly when mixing plants together or creating a display that has to last a number of years. Does the plant grow from a central cluster of shoots or does it spread by runners (like many cranesbill, *Geranium*) or by underground rhizomes (like some grasses)? Is the foliage attractive enough on its own, irrespective of flowers? Does the plant

blossom in one burst, or intermittently over the year? Does the plant fill out quickly or is it slow to bulk up? Will the plant stems require staking or tying in?

Grouping plants

In small containers, it is best to use one particular cultivar, as a single plant or in a clump of three. In larger containers – 45cm (18in) or more in diameter – you have more scope to mix plants. A large, mature specimen of a slower-growing, feature plant goes well with smaller specimens of faster-growing, supporting plants, but match the vigour of the plants to achieve a balanced effect.

Place a tall, upright plant in the centre or towards the back, with 1–3 supporting cultivars of smaller size around it. Trailing cultivars can be set around the rim, to cascade over the side. After planting, water and feed plants regularly (see p142, 146).

REFRESHING STOCK

Depending on the density of the planting and vigour of the cultivars, plantings may need breaking up and replanting each year or so to maintain vitality and replenish the potting compost. At that point the plantings can be revamped by introducing new plants.

• ANNUALS IN CONTAINERS •

Everyone loves flowers, and annual plants can really add floral piquancy to any potted display. They can be used in so many different ways: grown singly or in groups in plugs or small pots; they can be tucked in as highlights in a longer-term, shrubby or perennial display; or you can design your own colour-themed planting, blending tones and hues for an exhilarating burst of colour, or creating something more demure or muted in effect. It is also easier to link your colour theme to an element in the surrounding garden or architecture feature, and choose an annual(s) that will resonate with it.

VERSATILE ANNUALS

The wonderful thing, too, is that you can change the planting the following year with little cost or inconvenience if something does not quite work visually or you want to ring the changes and try something completely different. Annuals need not be a one-hit wonder, either. Many are long-flowering or have interesting seedheads, prolonging the

SOWING A MEADOW IN A POT

There are many mixtures available to create a variety of effects. Carry out seed sowing in spring on a day with calm weather, to avoid the wind whisking your seed mixture away. Fill the container with damp, peat-free potting compost and create a level seedbed. If the compost is coarse, fill gaps with sieved compost or a layer of horticultural sand. After sowing (see p124), water the seed. If you are worried that birds might disturb the seedbed, cover the pot with horticultural fleece. Once the seedlings have fully established, the fleece can be removed. Keep young plants moist, especially during hot or windy weather.

display still further. By sowing particular species and cultivars successively over a number of weeks, you can further prolong the length of display. You could also stage a display of everlasting flowers (including Bracteantha, Gomphrena, Helipterum, Limonium and Xeranthemum) with their fascinating papery petals, which you could pick and dry. Collect seed of your favourite annuals (not F1 hybrids) and save money.

ANNUAL MIXTURES

Why not experiment by mixing annuals together and sowing your own meadow seed mixtures with flaxes (*Linum*), poppies (*Papaver*), cornflowers (*Centaurea cyanus*) and marguerites (*Leucanthemum vulgare*) (see box on p95)? Or you can buy a wide range of ready mixed annuals

that have been tried and tested and will perform reliably for you. If you want that meadow-like effect, try including a few annual grasses, such as squirrel tail grass (*Hordeum jubatum*) or hare's tail (*Lagurus ovatus*). You could also even include a dwarf form of corn or barley.

HELPING WILDLIFE

If you choose single, open flowers, your display of annuals can become a food magnet for bees, butterflies and other pollinating insects. Many annuals produce copious amounts of pollen and nectar, which these organisms love.

TYPES OF ANNUAL

Annuals can be divided into three groups: hardy, half-hardy and tender perennials grown as annuals (see p122). There are also two main types of climber. Firstly, there are those that fulfil their life by growing and setting seed within a year, predominantly flowering in high summer and finishing by autumn. Secondly, there are perennial climbers from warm climates – which are tender in cool-temperate areas – such as black-

*A planter filled with a mixture of French marigolds (*Tagetes*) will provide colour and contrast all summer long.*

ANNUALS WITH A PURPOSE

Annuals for hot, dry conditions
Dimorphotheca (African daisy)
Euphorbia marginata
   (snow on the mountain)
Gaillardia pulchella (blanket flower)
Gomphrena globosa (globe amaranth)
Portulaca grandiflora (rose moss)
Rudbeckia hirta (black-eyed Susan)
Sanvitalia (creeping zinnia)
Verbena
Xeranthemum (everlasting flower)
Zinnia

Annuals for shady conditions
Begonia
Cleome (spider flower)
Impatiens (busy Lizzie)
Lobelia
Lobularia (sweet alyssum)
Mimulus (monkey flower)
Nemophila menziesii (baby blue-eyes)
Nicotiana (tobacco plant)
Torenia (wishbone flower)
Viola (violet)

Annuals with good seedheads
Helianthus annuus (sunflower)
Hordeum jubatum (squirrel tail grass)
Lagurus ovatus (hare's tail)
Moluccella laevis (bells of Ireland)
Nigella damascena (love-in-a-mist)
Papaver somniferum (opium poppy)
Rhodanthe (strawflower)

Scabiosa stellata (paper moon flower)
Setaria italica (millet)
Xerochrysum bracteatum Monstrosum
   Series (golden everlasting)

Perennials flowering their first year
   from seed
Achillea (yarrow)
Agastache (giant hyssop)
Coreopsis (tickseed)
Gaillardia (blanket flower)
Gaura (bee blossom)
Helenium (Helen's flower)
Lupinus (lupin)
Lychnis (catchfly)
Penstemon
Prunella (self-heal)

Rewarding annual climbers
Cardiospermum halicacabum
   (love in a puff)
Cobaea scandens (cup and saucer plant)
Eccremocarpus scaber
   (Chilean glory flower)
Ipomoea lobata (Spanish flag), *I. purpurea*
   (common morning glory)
Lathyrus odoratus (sweet pea)
Lophospermum (foxglove climber)
Rhodochiton atrosanguineus
   (purple bell vine)
Thunbergia alata (black-eyed Susan)
Tropaeolum peregrinum
   (canary creeper)

eyed Susan (*Thunbergia alata*), Chilean glory flower (*Eccremocarpus scaber*) and cup and saucer plant (*Cobaea scandens*). These latter type of climber tend to start flowering later and will often continue doing so until the first frosts cut them down. All annuals can be easily grown from seed or purchased by mail order as small plug plants (see p81).

USING ANNUAL CLIMBERS

Annual climbers are a gift for container gardeners as they can be planted to create height and drama in ways that other annuals simply cannot. Many are also spectacular in flower and can provide a long season of interest, particularly into late summer and autumn, and some,

Popular annual climbers to grow in containers include: Chilean glory flower (left), sweet pea (centre) and morning glory (right).

such as sweet peas (*Lathyrus odoratus*), have a delicious scent.

Grow one plant, perhaps in matching pots to flank a doorway or stairway, or try mixing 2–3 species or cultivars using the various shades of black-eyed Susan or sweet pea to create startling contrasts or elegant harmonies of tone.

You can also try mixing different climbers together: blue morning glory (*Ipomoea*) and orange Spanish flag (*I. lobata*) make a startling combination. They can also be used to fill gaps in larger container plantings, festooning the surrounding plants or to create height at the back of the container. With their root systems in the pot, they can also be used to clamber over adjacent structures such as an arbour or trellis canopy.

As most climb by twining they will require some form of support (see p150). You may also need initially to tie in the shoots to the support.

• ALPINES IN CONTAINERS •

You can always make room for a potted display of alpines, even if you have the tiniest space in which to garden. They are the jewels of the plant world, and their tolerance of arduous conditions makes them ideal for garden spaces that are unprotected and open to the elements: for example, for a roof garden.

Many plants are sold as alpines in garden centres, but often turn out to be anything but alpines, as they quickly expand to extinguish anything in their way. If possible, seek advice and purchase plants from a garden centre with a knowledgeable adviser or visit a specialist nursery.

DISPLAYING ALPINES

Alpines are usually grown together in small communities rather than in isolation, combining those with similar needs and modest growth habits, so they will not quickly swamp their neighbours. As the majority of alpines

In small containers choose alpines with restricted rates of growth, to prevent vigorous types from swamping others.

are shallow rooting, they require pots or containers that are wider than deep, such as clay pans or troughs. They look particularly effective in stone troughs, nestled among artfully placed rocks and gravel to emulate the look of their mountain homeland. Antique troughs

ALPINES WITH A PURPOSE

Dainty shrubs & conifers

Cotoneaster congestus 'Nanus'

Daphne cneorum 'Eximia', *D. retusa*

Hebe armstrongii, H. buchananii

Jasminum parkeri (jasmine)

Juniperus communis 'Compressa'

Linum arboreum (flax)

Penstemon menziesii, P. rupicola
　(rock penstemon)

Polygala chamaebuxus var. *grandiflora*
　(snakeroot)

Salix 'Boydii' (willow)

Beautiful bulbs

Allium mairei var. *amabile, A. cyathophorum*
　var. *farreri* (ornamental onion)

Cyclamen coum, C. hederifolium

Fritillaria michailovskyi, F. uva-vulpis (fritillary)

Iris danfordiae, I. histrioides, I. reticulata

Narcissus bulbicodium, N. juncifolius,

N. rupicola (daffodil)

Ornithogalum oligophyllum
　(star-of-Bethlehem)

Oxalis adenophylla (shamrock)

Rhodohypoxis baurii cvs

Triteleia ixioides

Tulipa batalinii, T. biflora, T. humilis

Plants with character

Armeria juniperifolia (thrift)

Campanula betulifolia, C. cochlearifolia
　'Elizabeth Oliver' (bellflower)

Dianthus alpinus, D. haematocalyx (pink)

Gentiana verna (star gentian)

Lewisia cotyledon hybrids

Morisia monanthos

Ramonda myconi

Saxifraga x *apiculata, S.* 'Edith',
　S. oppositifolia (saxifrage)

Sempervivum (houseleek) cvs

are now highly coveted, but there is a ready supply of modern facsimiles, which are cheaper and still retain the original look. Old ceramic sinks are also used for miniature alpine gardens and can be covered in hypertufa (see p30).

GROWING MEDIA FOR ALPINES

Most alpine plants thrive in soil that is low in certain nutrients, particularly nitrogen, and this regime needs to be adopted when putting together your potted alpine garden. Soil that is too rich will encourage the plants to grow too lushly, becoming overleafy and sappy. As well as losing their tight, compact charm, they become less resistant to attack by pests and diseases and the freezing conditions of winter, at which point they usually expire.

Always use a loam-based potting compost, such as John Innes No 1 (see box on p137) or a similar one blended for alpines. Some alpines, such as some gentians (*Gentiana*), are lime-intolerant and so need ericacaeous mix. All alpines require soil that is well drained, so mix a little extra grit into the potting compost, by up to a half measure by volume.

PLANTING ALPINES

Fill your container with the compost. If you plan to add any rocks to create a miniature landscape, position them as you add the compost and bed them in. By creating fissures between rocks, you can provide planting pockets for rosette plants, such as lewisia, ramonda and saxifrages (*Saxifraga*). Place taller alpines in the centre of the pot and creeping ones at the edge, so they can cascade over the sides. The compost surface should be 4cm (1$^{1}/_{2}$in) below the rim of the container so there

Most alpines require good drainage, so grow in a gritty potting compost and work a gravel mulch around plant necks.

is space to spread a 1cm ($^{1}/_{2}$in) layer of washed horticultural grit or gravel across the surface and beneath the collar of the plants. This not only improves visual appeal but also prevents water lodging around the plants (see p154).

If located in the open, most alpines need only periodic watering, usually during prolonged drought spells. Ideally, use soft water or collected rainwater, particularly if you live in a hard-water area. This is especially important when growing lime-intolerant plants. Avoid waterlogging plants (see box on p140). Alpines will benefit from a light annual application of a balanced, slow-release fertiliser (see p146). Keep a check on the health of your plants and snip off spent flowers and seedheads to help keep them tidy (see p158).

• HARDY CLIMBERS
IN CONTAINERS •

If you want height in a container and don't necessarily want to grow a tree or shrub, then climbers are an exciting and versatile option. Most flower beautifully and prodigiously, and many are also wonderfully scented. Hardy climbers that can be grown in containers span a diversity of plant types, from climbing roses (*Rosa*) to passion flowers (*Passiflora*).

WHAT TO GROW?

The main restriction governing what to grow is the usual one of pot size. The bigger the pot, the more vigorous and expansive type of climber you can grow, and the more space it will cover. If you can accommodate only a small pot, say less than 30cm (12in) in diameter, plant an annual climber. In a pot 30–35cm (12–14in) in diameter you have a bigger

CLEMATIS IN POTS

Clematis are the most rewarding, hardy climbers you can grow in a pot in terms of the size and number of their flowers. Almost all except the larger, more rampant species such as *C. montana* and most of their cultivars can happily be accommodated in a container for many years. Try, for example, diminutive and compact, late winter- and spring-flowering beauties such as cultivars of *C. x cartmanii* (right), *C. alpina* and *C. macropetala*, through to the larger, later-flowering hybrids. Some clematis, such as *C. tangutica* and *C. orientalis*, have mop-like seedheads that look sensational when coated in dew or frosted in haw.

CLIMBERS WITH A PURPOSE

Climbers for sun

Actinidia kolomikta
Ampelopsis
Clematis
Lonicera (honeysuckle)
Passiflora caerulea (blue passion flower)
Solanum crispum (Chilean potato tree)
Trachelospermum
Vitis 'Brant' (grapevine)

Climbers for shade

Akebia quinata (chocolate vine)
Celastrus scandens (American bittersweet)
Clematis alpina, *C. macropetala*
Euonymus fortunei
Hedera colchica (Persian ivy) cvs, *H. helix* (English ivy) cvs
Hydrangea anomala subsp. *petiolaris* (climbing hydrangea)
Jasminum nudiflorum (winter jasmine)
Lonicera × *brownii* (scarlet trumpet honeysuckle), *L.* × *tellmanniana*
Parthenocissus (Virginia creeper)

Climbers for scent

Akebia quinata 'Alba' (chocolate vine)
Clematis armandii, *C. flammula*
Jasminum officinale (common jasmine)
Lonicera caprifolium (Italian honeysuckle), *L. pericymenum* (woodbine)
Rosa (rose) – climbing and rambling
Schisandra grandiflora
Trachelospermum asiaticum

Long-/repeat-flowering clematis

C. 'Anita'
C. florida var. *florida* 'Sieboldiana'
C. 'Minuet'
C. 'Nelly Moser'
C. 'Vyvyan Pennell'
C. 'Warszawska Nike'

Clematis for shade

C. 'Alba Luxurians'
C. alpina and cvs
C. 'Bees' Jubilee'
C. 'Ernest Markham'
C. 'Marie Boisselot'
C. 'Nelly Moser'
C. 'Perle d'Azur'

Climbing roses for sun

R. 'Albertine'
R. 'Dreaming Spires'
R. Graham Thomas
R. 'New Dawn'
R. The Pilgrim
R. White Cloud

Climbing shade-tolerant roses

R. A Shropshire Lad (climbing)
R. 'Golden Showers'
R. Iceberg (climbing)
R. 'New Dawn'
R. 'Roseraie de l'Haÿ'
R. 'The Garland'
R. 'Zéphirine Drouhin'

WISTERIA IN POTS

Although wisteria is a vigorous climber, some cultivars are particularly accommodating for pot culture, such as W. floribunda 'Rosea' and W. frutescens 'Amethyst Falls'. The latter flowers a little later and not as densely or fragrantly as the more common Chinese wisteria (W. sinensis), but it is still very attractive. Chinese wisteria can be grown in a large urn, 60cm (2ft) or more in diameter and straight-sided, to provide as much root room as possible. All wisteria require a continual regime of training and pruning to establish a central woody framework strong enough to be self-supporting.

range of planting opportunities; most clematis and smaller, woody climbers such as jasmines (*Jasminum*) and honeysuckles (*Lonicera*) will be adequately accommodated. Larger, more vigorous climbers, such as wisteria, trumpet vine (*Campsis*), potato flower (*Solanum*) and many climbing roses, require pots at least 45cm (18in) in diameter.

Plant climbers in loam-based potting compost unless they are ericaceous (see p132). Water (see p142) and feed (see p146) the plants regularly, and keep them tidy (see p158).

SUPPORTING CLIMBERS

The structure will depend on the type of climber (see box on p135). Those with aerial roots (e.g. *Hydrangea anomala* subsp. *petiolaris*) or adhesive discs at the end of their tendrils (e.g. Virginia creeper/*Parthenocissus*) require a stout, freestanding trellis to grow up or can be attached to an adjacent wall or pergola. Twining climbers (such as honeysuckle) spiral up their support. Many of the larger climbers (such as rambling roses) tend to clamber over things, rather than twine, and so will need to be tied into place either up their own supports or over an adjacent structure (see p150). These vigorous climbers will need their shoots thinned and occasionally unruly or wayward growth removed to keep them under control (see p160).

DISENTANGLING CLIMBERS

Once a woody or evergreen climber has attached itself to a structure, such as an arbour or pergola, it is likely to be difficult to repot and may require being cut back hard to detach the plant before the rootball can be extracted from the pot. A few climbers will sulk after such hard pruning, but they generally recover over time. Flowering may be affected for at least a year after hard pruning.

• CACTI & SUCCULENTS IN CONTAINERS •

Many cacti and succulents are easy and rewarding to grow, their main requirements being full sun, well-drained potting compost and care in not overfeeding or overwatering them, because they are prone to rotting and attack by various pests and diseases. Almost all cacti and succulents from warm climes need overwintering under glass, but they can be put out for the summer. Start to withdraw watering in midautumn, so they dry

CACTI & SUCCULENTS TO TRY UNDER GLASS

Cacti
Astrophytum
Cephalocereus
Echinocereus
Echinopsis
Gymnocalycium
Mammillaria
Parodia
Rebutia

Succulents
Adromischus
Aeonium

Aloe
Crassula
Echeveria
Euphorbia
(spurge)
Haworthia
Lithops (stone plant)
Sedum (stonecrop)
Stapelia (carrion flower)

For dry, sunny conditions succulents are unsurpassed, but ensure they are winter hardy before leaving them outdoors.

out before cold weather hits. Hardy succulents, such as many stonecrops (*Sedum*) and crassula can be kept outside all year round. Most cacti and succulents can be grown in John Innes No 1 potting compost (see box on p137), with horticultural grit added for drainage. When in active growth, water when the compost has dried out; each month feed with a special, low-nitrogen fertiliser with extra trace elements.

• ORCHIDS IN CONTAINERS •

In recent years, thanks to the work of breeders, a range of tropical orchids have become popular house plants. Now, moth orchids (*Phalaenopsis*) and others such *Dendrobium* can be found in many shops and are highly decorative plants for windowsills, well-lit rooms and conservatories; they flower profusely over many weeks, if not months. These orchids are known as epiphytes (plants growing on others, usually trees, without obtaining food from them), and they need to be grown in ways that mimic their native conditions.

Although bought in pots, in the wild epiphytic orchids are found growing on rocks or in the crotches or along the branches of trees, their roots binding them to crevices and nooks and crannies, which are often filled with humus formed from decaying leaves and other forest detritus. Many of these types of orchid have adapted to withstand periodic drought.

CONTAINERS FOR EPIPHYTES

Epiphytic orchids such as phalaenopsis can be grown in unglazed, terracotta pots or in open-slatted baskets suspended from a window frame. Other epiphytes such as vanda are best in tall, large glass jars, with their roots devoid of compost and completely exposed. Smaller orchids are often displayed in brandy balloons or wine glasses, where they need to be carefully watered to avoid waterlogging them.

GROWING EPIPHYTES

Orchid composts for epiphytes are usually a mix of bark chips and other elements such as charcoal chips and coarse perlite or hydroleca (superheated clay minerals) which, although retaining some moisture, are very quick draining and poor in nutrients. These are supplied to the plant by spraying once a month in the growing season with a liquid orchid fertiliser, which is low in nitrogen and high in phosphates and other micronutrients.

Ideally, epiphytic orchids should be watered with rainwater rather than tap

ORCHIDS UNDER GLASS

Coelogyne	Phalaenopsis
Dendrobium	(moth orchid)
Masdevallia	Vanda
Paphiopedilum	
(slipper orchid)	

water, especially in hard-water areas. Water the plants weekly during the flowering and growing period, but allow the plants to drain and slightly dry out before adding more.

Maintain a minimum temperature of 15°C (59°F), and avoid plants being exposed to huge swings in temperature or cold draughts, especially when sited on windowsills. They require bright, indirect sunlight; direct, hot sun can scorch both the leaves and roots. Although best in humid conditions under glass, some hardier epiphytic orchids can be placed outside for the summer, but do not place them in exposed positions in direct sunlight.

Orchids such as miltonia, miltoniopsis *and* phalaenopsis *make excellent house plants, given warmth and good light.*

ORCHIDS FOR OUTDOORS

There are a few terrestrial orchids, such as calanthe, that can be grown in pots in shady locations. These orchids need to be grown in a loam-based potting compost, such as John Innes No 2 (see box on p137), to which is added shredded or chipped bark and charcoal chips. Keep them out of direct sun and ensure they are moist at all times, again preferably using rainwater. In cool-temperate areas, they may need protection in winter.

· TENDER EXOTICS IN CONTAINERS ·

Tropical and subtropical plants have long held a fascination for gardeners. They collectively comprise a varied mixture of shrubby, evergreen perennial or bulbous plants that often possess large leaves and/or richly coloured flowers displayed to create spectacular effects. Such plants were very popular throughout the Victorian and Edwardian era, even though they required glasshouse protection in winter; they were bedded out for the summer. Their cultivation was expensive, and their popularity declined in the changed social climate of the 20th century.

NEW POPULARITY

However, tender exotics are once again fashionable and now widely available. Use them to create flamboyant summer and autumn displays in large tubs and other containers, either as feature plants on their own or in association with other ornamentals, such as Indian shot plant (*Canna*), coleus (*Solenostemon*) and fuchsia, or summer bedding plants (see p13).

Combine palms, succulents and large-leaved evergreen and deciduous plants to create your own subtropical jungle.

Bananas (Musa) will grow luxuriantly if given enough root room, plenty of moisture and feed; they do need winter protection.

One great advantage of tropical and subtropical plants is that they can be discarded at the end of the year and subsequently repurchased for the following year. Alternatively, if perennial, they can be given the protection of a glasshouse or conservatory over winter and be used again next season. Cut back overlarge plants or propagate them from cuttings or by division, as required. Bulbous plants, such as Indian shot plant, caladium and ginger lily (*Hedychium*), can be dried off after they have finished, old foliage allowed to wither or removed and then be stored dry in frost-free conditions.

GROWING TIPS

Those plants from warmer and more humid climates require a warm, sheltered spot, such as a south- or southwest-facing wall, to do well outdoors in cool-temperate areas.

Depending on location and local growing conditions, some exotics, such as the tree fern dicksonia or Chusan palm (*Trachycarpus fortunei*), may be hardy or of borderline hardiness,

requiring some shelter and protection to get them through winter. These types of plants will always be at risk from damage or being killed by low temperatures, so be prepared to have substitutes or periodically repurchase them.

Most exotic plants used as summer bedding grow well in a peat-free, multipurpose potting compost, and they also benefit from copious moisture and rich feeding (see pp142, 146).

Begonias In subtropical displays, begonias are often taller, 'cane-stemmed' or 'angel-winged' species and cultivars, such as *B. albopicta* (guinea-wing begonia), 1–1.5m (3–5ft) tall, with its mass of pale pink flowers and silver-spotted foliage; smaller *B. rex* has brightly or boldly patterned leaves.

Caladium (Angel wings) Tuberous perennials, 30–60cm (1–2ft) tall, from South America, with spectacular, multicoloured, arrow-shaped leaves. Needs humidity and shelter, as leaves are sensitive to drying winds and heavy rain.

Dicksonia antarctica (Soft tree fern) Hardiest and most commonly available tree fern. Mature plants have filigree fronds, 1.8–2.5m (6–8ft) long, on top of stout 'trunk' composed of roots and old leaf bases. Grow in half-barrel or large tub in moist, ericaceous compost, siting in shelter, in semi- to full shade. Keep 'trunks' moist and avoid cold, drying winds. Provide cold protection to growing point and 'trunk' in winter.

Musa (Banana) and **Ensete** Evergreen, palm-like perennials, 1.8m (6ft) tall, with a stout stem composed of fleshy leafstalks and large, paddle-shaped leaves, some blotched red. Fabulous feature plants. Try *M. acuminata* 'Dwarf Cavendish', *M. basjoo* (Japanese banana), *M. sikkimensis* or *Ensete ventricosum* 'Maurelii' (Ethiopian

banana). Best lifted and overwintered in frost-free conditions.

Palms Ideal plants for larger containers. Some are hardy, but protect from freezing snow. *Trachycarpus fortunei* (Chusan palm), 3.7m (12ft) tall, or compact *T. wagnerianus* are the hardiest and best. *Chamaerops humilis* (dwarf fan palm) can be killed in hard winters; *C.h.* var. *argentea* has blue leaves, while *C.h.* 'Vulcano' is dwarf. Overwinter *Phoenix canariensis* (Canary Island date palm) indoors.

Plectranthus (Spurflower) Shrubby, evergreen perennials, 15–90cm (6–36in) tall, from Africa, India, Indonesia and Australia, with slender spikes of blue, purple or mauve flowers and attractive, aromatic foliage. *P. argentatus* bears large, velvety, silvered leaves; *P. verticillatus* (Swedish ivy) has rounded, variegated leaves and prostrate habit; ideal for hanging baskets.

Solanum (Potato flower) Hardy to tender, woody shrubs or small trees, to 1.8m (6ft) or more, with showy, blue-purple or white flowers; some also with attractive foliage. Look out for *S. crispum* (Chilean potato tree), *S. laciniatum*

Stems of evergreen blue potato bush (Lycianthes rantonnetii) can be trained and pruned into a globe-headed standard.

Glory bush is an upright, strongly branched shrub, and makes an ideal centrepiece of a large, subtropical display.

(kangaroo apple) and *S. laxum* 'Album' (potato vine).

Streptosolon jamesonii (Marmalade bush) Gawky, evergreen shrubs, 0.9–1.8m (3–6ft) tall, from Andean woodland. Loose clusters of flowers open orange, then fade to yellow. Long-flowered, making it a good filler plant.

Tetrapanax (Ricepaper plant) Evergreen shrubs, 1.8m (6ft) tall, with enormous serrated leaves. Protect in winter; new growth will sprout from roots if top growth is killed.

Tibouchina urvilleana (Glory bush) Evergreen shrubs, 1.2–2.5m (4–8ft) tall, from Brazil, with strongly veined leaves. Electric blue, chalice-shaped flowers throughout summer. Can be pruned to size and shape. Dwarf forms also available.

Xanthosoma (Elephant's ear) Sumptuous, leafy perennials, 0.6–1.2m (2–4ft) or more tall, from tropical America. Foliage is usually arrow shaped, often toned red or purple from a central corm. Dry plant off in autumn and overwinter in frost-free conditions.

• CONTAINER RECIPES •

ROSES IN A COUNTRY GARDEN

Many roses (*Rosa*) perform to perfection in pots, particularly if you choose compact cultivars or those that rebloom or blossom over a long season and keep them fed and watered. If planning to combine them with fast-growing annuals or perennials, it pays to establish the rose in the container for a year or two, so it is substantial enough to compete. Specimens with tall, leggy stems also allow other plants to be more easily grown beneath. Opposite, an opulent planting of apricot English rose 'Grace' is combined with other pastel-shaded flowers in pink, lilac and violet from drought-tolerant and long-flowering *Scabiosa* Burgundy Bonnets, 'Lilac Haze' verbena and tall airy *Verbena bonariensis*. Swags of trailing pale peach begonia and chocolate vine (*Rhodochiton atrosanguineum*) drape over the side of the container to extend the time of interest. All perennials are best removed and fresh stock replanted each year, so that the rose is not overwhelmed.

Planting palette
- Begonia 'Million Kisses Elegance'
- Rhodochiton atrosanguineus (chocolate vine)
- Rosa 'Grace' (English rose)
- Scabiosa Burgundy Bonnets (pincushion flower)
- Verbena bonariensis
- Verbena rigida f. lilacina 'Lilac Haze'

WINTER SHAPE & SCENT

When the riotous splendour of summer is over, bring winter to life with pots of evergreens shrubs and perennials, whose leaf shapes, colours and textures can be used to powerful effect. A bright yellow ling heather (*Calluna*) and silver-veined coral flower (*Heuchera*) vividly contrast with dark green skimmia and sweet box (*Sarcococca hookerana* var. *digyna*) (see p114), while a sculptural polypody fern provides a splash of fresh green. Long-lasting flowers from the skimmia add visual spice, while the small, white flowers of the sweet box provide a welcome, delicate scent. The pot would be suitable sited in either sun or semishade in winter, but may need shadier conditions during summer. When densely planted for instant effect,

Roses in a country garden *Reblooming or long-flowered roses work best in containers, and look great when mingling to luxuriant effect with airy sprays of other flowers.*

112

some plants such as the fern may need removing or the container replanted in due course.

Planting palette

- *Calluna vulgaris* 'Yellow Beauty' (ling)
- *Heuchera sanguinea* 'Geisha's Fan' (coral bells)
- *Polypodium vulgare* (common polypody)
- *Sarcococca hookerana* var. *digyna* (sweet box)
- *Skimmia japonica* 'Rubella'

CREATIVE COTTAGE GARDEN SPLENDOUR

Resplendent in a recycled, galvanized tub (see p115), the elegant reblooming rose (*Rosa* The Lady's Blush) revels in the sun, producing a succession of semidouble, pink, yellow-centred chalices over fresh green foliage. The companion planting is simple and also long-flowering. Seed-raised tufts of jazzy purple-net toadflax (*Linaria reticulata* 'Flamenco') are tucked into vacant gaps and soon burst into their dazzling, two-toned display, while a skirt of brooding *Verbena* 'Homestead Purple' cascades over the side, attracting both bees and butterflies. The toadflax can be allowed to self-seed to provide another show for no effort, or be removed when exhausted so you can try something new and exciting. All roses in containers will benefit from fresh compost and a little balanced fertiliser

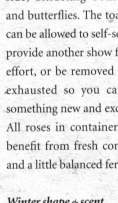

Winter shape & scent
Evergreens are the mainstay of winter containers, their leaves often becoming burnished or brighter in cold weather.

Creative cottage garden splendour
Relaxed plantings of rose and riotous annuals in an old washtub combine to provide a contemporary twist on the cottage-garden theme.

the wealth of compact, dark-leaved cultivars now available. The range of flower colours is astonishing, from demure pastels to screaming vibrant hues. Here (see p116), soft yellow *D.* 'Clarion' has been married with blue *Hebe* 'Royal Blue' and a few bedding asters to great effect. Autumnal highlights are provided by the grass *Miscanthus oligostachyus* 'Afrika' with its attractive flowerheads and red-tinted foliage deepening as the season progresses. Old flower stems of hebe are removed when spent and the herbaceous miscanthus is cut back in late winter. The tender dahlia tuber will require lifting and storing in autumn, replanting it the following season, while the aster can be replaced with other seasonal bedding plants.

being applied in early spring; this is also the time when any pruning should be carried out, such as pruning to shape or thinning overcrowded stems (see p160).

Planting palette

- *Linaria reticulata* 'Flamenco' (purple-net toadflax)
- *Rosa* The Lady's Blush (rose)
- *Verbena* 'Homestead Purple'

TAKING DELIGHT IN DAHLIAS

Dahlias are among the most invaluable summer-flowering plants for the container gardener, particularly with

Taking delight in dahlias A sea of blue blossom contrasted with the pale yellow stars of Dahlia 'Clarion' illustrate a restrained, yet powerful use of colour.

Being creative with sempervivum With myriad forms to choose from, the rosettes of succulent houseleeks can be used to create living tapestries of colour.

Planting palette
- *Aster dumosus* hybrid (New York aster)
- *Dahlia* 'Clarion'
- *Hebe* 'Royal Blue'
- *Miscanthus oligostachyus* 'Afrika'

BEING CREATIVE WITH SEMPERVIVUM

For hot, dry, sunny conditions, houseleeks (*Sempervivum*) are unsurpassed, thriving where many plants would be severely stressed. They are a very useful group of hardy, succulent plants requiring little care, save for an occasional watering, making them ideal for absentee container owners. They are also strangely addictive and easily collected as the leaves in each compact rosette come in a wide range of shapes and patterns (*S.* 'Bronco' is red, *S. giuseppii* red-tipped) or are covered in hairs or webbed in silken thread (*S.* 'Petite Renée'). Mature rosettes extend to produce a short stem with pink, star-like flowers, but die after flowering. Grow in well-drained, loam-based potting compost, such as John Innes No 1 (see box on p137), adding extra grit for drainage. Most are easily propagated by detaching offsets, which quickly root where placed. Here (see left), pots have been tiered inside each other on layers of compost and the margins planted with contrasting cultivars to great effect.

Planting palette

- *Sempervivum* 'Bronco' (houseleek)
- *Sempervivum giuseppii* (houseleek)
- *Sempervivum* 'Petite Renée' (houseleek)

MOUNTAIN JEWELS ON DISPLAY

Alpine plants come from a wide range of high-altitude environments, and when carefully chosen you can create a plant display for

Mountain jewels on display
For those with tiny spaces such as balconies, containers full of alpines offer a wonderful way to create gardens in miniature.

sun or semishade. Being diminutive, alpines are also suitable for staging an attractive display of pots, troughs and raised beds in the smallest garden spaces. The arrangement of alpines here (see below) is ideal for a sunny position. Plants such as phlox, pinks (*Dianthus*) and tanacetum are mat- or hummock-forming, while the houseleek (*Sempervivum*) produces a cluster of fleshy rosettes. When wanting to grow alpines together, choose those with similar restrictive or slow-growth habits, to prevent any one from swamping the others. Being shallow or sparsely rooted, alpines are best grown in shallow pans or troughs and in well-drained, gritty, loam-based potting compost.

117

Planting palette
- *Dianthus* 'Blue Hills' (pink)
- *Phlox subulata*
- *Sempervivum arachnoideum* (houseleek)
- *Sempervivum* 'King George' (houseleek)
- *Tanacetum densum* subsp. *amani*

SUNFLOWERS TO CELEBRATE SUMMER

Sunflowers are one of the delights of late summer and always lift the spirits. You don't often see them mixed together, but in a large container you can create an impressive display. All the plants in this arrangement (see opposite) were grown from seed sown in early spring, potted on and planted out in a container, 60cm (2ft) wide, in late spring. Pick a sunny but sheltered spot away from damaging winds. One or two plants of 'Claret' sunflowers (*Helianthus annuus*) were planted in the centre, with three or four plants of the smaller and weaker *H.* 'Key Lime Pie' planted around them. Remaining gaps were planted with purple-leaved and -flowered *Amaranthus* 'Velvet Curtains' and white-flowered, double *Cosmos* 'Snow Puff' and spider plant

(*Cleome hassleriana* 'Helen Campbell'). Red and blue verbena added a colourful cascade around the edge. The secret to a large-flowered, leafy display is constant moisture, regular feeding and staking and tying in the stems to keep them upright. Remove any old foliage that becomes too unwieldy as plants develop.

Planting palette
- *Amaranthus cruentus* 'Velvet Curtains' (purple amaranth)
- *Cleome hassleriana* 'Helen Campbell' (spider plant)
- *Cosmos bipinnatus* 'Snow Puff'
- *Helianthus annuus* 'Claret' (sunflower)
- *Helianthus debilis* 'Key Lime Pie' (sunflower)
- *Verbena* Temari Blue
- *Verbena* Temari Red

Sunflowers to celebrate summer
Bold and sumptuous, a mass planting of sunflowers and other annuals provide a thrilling fanfare to announce summer's end.

CONTAINER
PRACTICALS

Annuals are among the most invaluable and diverse range of plants used in container gardening, and they are the mainstay of most floral displays. In terms of their life cycle and needs, annuals can be divided into three groups: hardy, half-hardy and tender perennials grown as annuals.

Hardy annuals

These are the true annuals that are cold- and frost-tolerant. They are sown in summer or autumn of the previous year, grown on in pots and planted out in their final positions in late autumn or late winter; they flower from early spring onwards. Hardy annuals can also be sown in late winter and planted out in spring, for flowers from early summer. Successional sowings 2–4 weeks apart will lengthen the floral display.

Half-hardy annuals

This term covers a mixture of plant types from short-lived annuals that are not cold-tolerant to frost-tender perennials and climbers that will flower the same year they are sown. Seeds of these plants are sown in spring under glass, grown on and hardened off for planting outdoors after the danger of late frost has passed;

this is usually in late spring. The bulk of these plants will flower from summer through to the first frosts of autumn. Again, successional sowing will extend the floral display. Most of the tender perennials can be overwintered under glass and reused the following season.

Tender perennials, grown as annuals

This group contains all the tender shrubs, perennials and climbers that are predominantly raised from cuttings and often sold by mail order as plug or small potted plantlets. They come from warmer climes, and if conditions are good, are often in flower for a prolonged period. They can eventually form sizeable, soft-wooded shrubs or climbers and can be lifted and overwintered to be grown on again the following season. They can also be used for cuttings.

PLANTING ANNUALS

Displays of annuals can be raised by two methods. The first and most frequently used is by sowing seed under glass, growing plants on and planting them out into containers when established. This is the safest method of producing sizeable plants. The second method is to sow seed directly

122

into the final container. This is particularly useful where the whole container is given over to annuals, particularly mixtures of wild flowers, and is the most reliable sowing method for hardy annuals. The germination of half-hardy annuals

The diversity of hardy and half-hardy annuals will open many new horizons for creative gardeners.

requiring higher temperatures may be affected by prevailing weather.

• GROWING ANNUALS •

Annuals are some of the easiest plants to raise from seed, but how and when will be determined by which of the three groups they fall into (see p122). Always read any cultural information on the packet before sowing.

SOWING SEED

Sow hardy and half-hardy annuals in pots, celltrays or half-trays. Fill containers to within 2.5cm (1in) of the rim with seed compost, then firm the compost lightly with a presser, (such as a flat piece of wood), to create a seedbed. Open the packet and hold it 2.5cm (1in) above the surface and at a 30-degree angle. Move your hand slowly over the compost allowing the seeds to fall evenly on the surface.

Most seeds require covering with potting compost. Fill a fine sieve with compost, then shake it, distributing a thin layer so that the compost just obscures the seeds. Finer seeds can be left uncovered. Bed seeds in with the presser, and label pots. Large-seeded annuals, such as nasturtium (*Tropaeolum majus*), can be sown individually or in small groups.

Water seeds using a fine rose, or soak trays from below. Place them on a bench and cover with a sheet of glass or a sealed,

SOWING IN POTS

Create a level seedbed. Sow evenly, just covering seed with sieved potting compost and water in. Cover with glass or a sealed, clear plastic bag while seeds germinate.

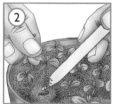

When large enough to handle by the seed leaf, transfer each seedling to a small pot or to a space in a celltray to grow on. Keep the potting compost moist while plants establish.

SOWING IN CELLTRAYS

Fill celltrays with potting compost. Sow large seeds individually, or smaller seeds sparingly in each module. Water in and cover till seeds germinate.

Grow plants on, thinning out seedlings to leave one in each module. Pot off each plantlet once its roots fill the module.

clear plastic bag, or place in a propagator. Maintain the temperature required for germination (see seed packet for details), checking with a thermometer. In hot weather shade with a sheet of newspaper. Remove the glass or propagator lid as seedlings appear and grow on.

PRICKING OUT

When large enough to handle by their seed leaves, transfer each seedling to a cell in a 15-unit celltray, or to a 6cm (2¹/₄in) pot. Fill celltrays or pots with compost, then create a hole for each seedling. Then gently extract a bundle of seedlings, and carefully tease apart. Insert the root of each seedling in a hole, firm with compost and water in. Tiny plants, such as lobelia, can be extracted and grown on as patches of seedlings.

As plants develop, pinch out the growth point to form a bushier plant.

BUYING BEDDING PLANTS

Many of the various types of plants grown as annuals can be bought from garden centres or by mail order already established in trays of variously sized plugs or cells of compost (see p81). Those bought by mail order are encased in protective packaging. Remove this on receipt and pot up plants and water in

Acclimatise plants raised under glass for planting in the open garden by hardening off in a cold frame for 14 days, gradually increasing ventilation and exposure to outdoor temperatures.

125

as soon as practicable. Feed occasionally with liquid fertiliser to boost growth.

HARDENING OFF

Plants, particularly tender annuals, need acclimatising to outdoor conditions. Two to four weeks before planting out, either transfer to a cold frame or reduce temperatures in the glasshouse by ventilation or place plants outdoors during warmer days, returning them at night. Plant out half-hardy annuals once the danger of late frost has passed.

• BULBS IN POTS •

Bulbs can provide interest in pots all year round, although are most associated with winter and spring. They are versatile and can be used to provide displays on their own or to fill gaps in mixed plantings for a splash of colour. The floral effect of bulbs, although enchanting, can frequently be fleeting. Their foliage is largely unattractive and soon deteriorates, so bulbs are usually removed after flowering and substituted by other plants to continue the display.

Plan bulb displays in advance. By choosing early or late cultivars you can enjoy a succession of flowers.

TIMELY PLANTINGS

Getting bulbs to perform successfully is all about timing. Bulbs need sufficient time to produce roots to support the huge effort of flowering. This means they should be planted some time in advance of when they are needed. As a general rule of thumb, plant spring bulbs from late summer into autumn, and plant summer bulbs from late autumn into spring.

PERMANENT PLANTINGS

You may wish to keep some types of bulbs as long-term plantings for their ornamental value or expense. Typical types might include cultivars of snowdrop (*Galanthus*), iris, miniature daffodils (*Narcissus*), tulips (*Tulipa*) or cyclamen. These require containers dedicated to them as they are likely to be swamped if grown with other vigorous perennials. Use loam-based potting compost, mixing in a little horticultural grit for drainage.

MASSING DISPLAYS

Bulbs of different kinds can be planted together to provide a mass of flowers appearing simultaneously or a succession of flowers over a period of time – a technique known as layer planting (see box on p83). Marry different-coloured crocuses, daffodils or tulips together, or mix early and late daffodils. With careful selection and sufficient space you can enjoy bulbs that flower over many weeks, starting with crocuses, then daffodils, then tulips, then early ornamental onions (*Allium*).

CHOOSING BULBS

As you need plants that really perform, always purchase high-quality bulbs as soon as they are available. Avoid cheap deals containing poor specimens and bulbs stored in overheated shops. Also check bulbs for signs of fungal disease, and test they are firm and plump to the touch. When buying bulbs in pots, purchase when in growth or in bud to avoid disappointment.

127

TOP BULBS AND WHEN TO PLANT

Agapanthus campanulatus (African lily) – early spring

Canna indica – midspring

Crocosmia masoniorum (montbretia) – early spring

Crocus speciosus – early autumn

Cyclamen hederifolium – early summer

Erythronium grandiflorum – midautumn

Eucomis comosa (pineapple flower) – midspring

Fritillaria meleagris (snake's head fritillary) – midautumn

Galanthus elwesii (snowdrop) – early autumn

Gladiolus dalenii – midspring

Lilium regale – midautumn

Muscari armeniacum (grape hyacinth) – early autumn

Narcissus obvallaris (Tenby daffodil) – early autumn

Narcissus pseudonarcissus (wild daffodil) – early autumn

Nerine bowdenii – midsummer

Scilla siberica (Siberian squill) – early autumn

Tigridia pavonia (tiger flower) – midspring

Tulipa greigii (Greigii Group tulip) – midautumn

Zantedeschia aethiopica (arum lily) – early spring

PLANTING DEPTHS

As a general principle, plant bulbs under the same depth of compost as the bulb height (see box on p129). Always plant them with the shoot or bud uppermost. Most bulbs and corms are flask- or disc-shaped, with a pronounced point or nose (the growing tip) and a flat base from which roots emerge. Tubers, such as dahlias, have a central bud around which the swollen roots hang, while begonias have a round-bottomed disc and a central growth point. Lilies (*Lilium*) form concentric rings of fleshy leaves around the central bud.

PREPOTTED DISPLAYS

Bulbs can be planted directly into the container in advance, or you can plant them individually or in clusters in larger pots at the appropriate time and transfer them to final positions when they start into growth or are even just about to flower. Pots can either be removed or kept on, depending on the length of time the bulbs reside in the container. Tender bulbs, such as tuberous begonia, planted out for the summer can be started under glass in spring and transferred outdoors once the danger of frost has passed.

PLANTING TIPS

The majority of bulbs planted on their own will grow happily in most types of potting compost as long as it is free draining. Place bulbs at the requisite depth (see box on p129). Bulbs such as crocuses, daffodils and tulips can be packed quite closely, leaving 1–2.5cm ($^1/_2$–1in) between them.

If doing a massed bulb display, plan the planting beforehand, carefully estimating how many bulbs are required to fill the space and create the effect you want. You can have a taller bulb underplanted by a smaller one; with this, the bulbs are planted evenly throughout. With taller bulbs in the centre graduating to smaller bulbs at the edge, plant in concentric rings. Start by positioning the largest bulbs (which require the deepest planting) and finish with the smallest ones. Fill vacant spaces between larger bulbs with potting compost before positioning the next variety. Bulbs can again be packed closely together, and the smaller bulbs placed in gaps between the larger ones.

Label the position of the various species or cultivars before covering them over with compost and firming in between each bulb. Water the pots in thoroughly and keep moist while bulbs

BULB HEIGHT & PLANTING DEPTHS

Bulbs come in many shapes and sizes, but whatever their size the rule of thumb is to plant them as deep as the bulb is long, and to space them far enough apart that there is enough room for the foliage to expand fully. Larger bulbs, such as gladioli, lilies and dahlia, produce tall stems and large flowers, which are liable to wind damage and so benefit from being staked (see p150).

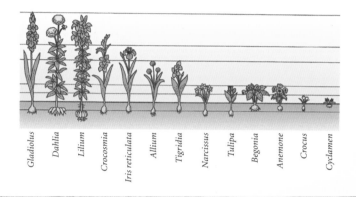

1.2m (4ft)

80cm (32in)

60cm (24in)

25cm (10in)
13cm (5in)
Soil line
13cm (5in)
deep

Gladiolus • Dahlia • Lilium • Crocosmia • Iris reticulata • Allium • Tigridia • Narcissus • Tulipa • Begonia • Anemone • Crocus • Cyclamen

establish and produce roots. Place in a shady position during winter, moving the pot into a sunny spot when buds appear. Apply an occasional liquid feed, using a high-potash fertiliser, once flower buds have formed (see p146).

BULB AFTERCARE

Once bulbs have flowered, remove their spent heads, as the next wave of bulbs grasp the limelight. When all bulbs have finished flowering either dispose of them and refresh stock next time, or else nurture them for use in another year. Allow foliage to wither naturally and then retrieve the bulbs. Alternatively, while still in leaf, remove the bulb from its pot and replant it in a nursery bed, where it can die down.

Firm compost at the required planting depth and space bulbs evenly. Label them so you remember them when they are dormant.

CONTAINER PRACTICALS

• PERENNIALS IN POTS •

Many hardy herbaceous and evergreen perennials are just as effective in pots as they are in the open garden.

VERSATILE USE

Perennials can be grown as single specimens or be massed together with other perennials and ornamental plants to create captivating and long-lasting displays of flower and foliage. Growing plants singly in pots attractively grouped together enables them to be grown to

perfection, without compromising individual cultivation needs and growth habits. Grown together, size and growth habit must be carefully matched. Some perennials are quick growing or spreading, while others are much slower and are soon overwhelmed by more robust neighbours. Also, select plants of similar age and size, to provide complementary levels of impact. Space plants so they have room to expand and produce more flowering shoots.

Perennials that require no staking are particularly useful; support those that are weaker stemmed or heavier flowered (see p150).

PERENNIAL CARE

Feed and water regularly (see pp142, 146). Deadhead flowers to keep plants neat (see p158) and to encourage new ones to form, unless they are late-

Grouping individual pots of plants such as hosta enables them to be grown to perfection and arranged to various effect.

Divide hostas in spring by cutting the crown to remove sections containing four or five rooted buds or shoots.

flowering perennials and grasses with flowerheads that provide attractive displays over winter, particularly when frosted. Pick over foliage plants, removing old and decaying leaves so the plants look tidy. Cut down the growth of deciduous perennials to ground level in late winter. Selectively remove old woody shoots or trim back stems of evergreen perennials, such as *Euphorbia characias*, after the flowerheads have deteriorated.

DIVIDING PERENNIALS

As herbaceous perennials expand, their centres often become woody and less productive. To reinvigorate the plants, lift and divide them every 2–4 years. To do this, remove the plant from its container when dormant, in late autumn or late winter. Shake off excess compost. Grab each side of the rootball and start to tear it apart; it will divide into small chunks. Some perennials may need severing with secateurs or prising apart with a couple of hand forks placed back to back and inserted into the gap. Select the strongest and most vigorous clumps for replanting. Some clumps of herbaceous perennials can be divided still further and the small plantlets grown on in a nursery bed to provide future stock. Plant new clumps into fresh compost and water in.

OVERWINTERING PERENNIALS

Tender perennials unlikely to withstand the rigours of winter outdoors can be moved for overwintering in a frost-free place, such as a glasshouse, conservatory or protected place outdoors. Provide such outdoor protection by mulching around the plant with dry straw or coarse bark chips. If space allows cover plants with an individual cloche for further protection and to keep off winter wet.

• WOODY PLANTS IN POTS •

Trees and shrubs in containers are long-lasting features, so from the outset provide them with the best possible conditions in which to grow and develop.

SELECTING WOODY PLANTS

Choose plants that are young, vigorous and healthy. Avoid those that have excessive weed growth in their pot or have weak or restricted new growth. Such plants are also likely to be pot-bound, which might hinder their quick and effective establishment. If possible remove the pot to inspect the rootball before purchase.

Trees and shrubs can also be bought bare root when dormant in winter. They require potting soon after purchase, and taller specimens will need staking (see p134). Always check the suitability and growing requirements of plants before purchasing (see p86). Some such as many members of the heather family (Ericaceae), like rhododendrons and heathers, require acid potting compost. Other plants grown in association with them will need to be compatible. Also check that the plants are suitable for their intended location, that is, shade-loving shrubs should be grown in

shade, not in full sun; and sun-lovers in sun, not shade.

CORRECT POT SIZE

Before planting a tree or shrub ensure its pot is large enough to accommodate the desired height and spread of the plant, and is deep enough for it to form a good root system; container cultivation will, however, naturally restrict the growth of larger species and cultivars. Containers should be broad and heavy enough to provide stability for tall specimens, which are liable to blow over in strong wind. Most shrubs should have 15cm (6in) of additional root space each time they are potted on (see p148), and trees need 15–30cm (6–12in) extra.

POTTING TECHNIQUES

Water the plant before potting it; if the compost is very dry, soak the rootball in a bucket of water. Add a layer of coarse gravel or stones to the bottom of the container, for drainage, then fill it with compost, lightly firming to a level that

When combining plants, such as these clematis and pansies, ensure the container is wide and deep enough.

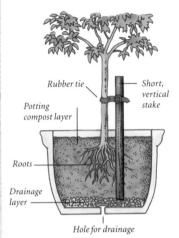

CONTAINER-GROWN TREE

Rubber tie

Potting
compost layer

Short,
vertical
stake

Roots

Drainage
layer

Hole for drainage

Support a freshly planted tree with a short stake for the first couple of years to prevent it from being blown over by strong winds. Remove the stake once the tree has become established.

as a stake, until they are established to prevent them being blown over or out of position by strong wind. Stakes can be either tall (supporting the entire trunk or stem) or short (providing support for the base and allowing the top of the tree to flex in the wind) (see box left). They should be 2.5–5cm (1–2in) in diameter.

While potting up the plant, position the stake about 7.5cm (3in) away from the trunk of the tree or shrub stem on the windward side, for maximum benefit. Secure the stem to the stake with a flexible rubber tie. If an extra strong support is required, hold the trunk between a tripod of stakes, again using rubber ties. Check ties frequently, and adjust to prevent them from unduly constricting or damaging the trunk.

would position the surface of the rootball about 5cm (2in) below the pot rim. Remove the original container from the plant to be potted on, and gently tease out some of the main roots from its rootball. Position the plant so it is both central and upright in the pot. Work in more compost, firming as you go, until the rootball is surrounded by fresh compost. Water the plant well and allow to drain.

STAKING TREES

Tall shrubs and especially trees are likely to need additional support, such

SUPPORTING CLIMBERS

The structure required will depend on the type and size of climber and the volume of growth it produces (see p150). Supports can vary from a few sprigs of brushwood or bamboo canes (slipped in and adjusted as climbers grow and develop) (see box right) through to sizeable, self-supporting trellis, which needs to be planned in from the outset.

Trellis varies in its robustness. Extendable trellis is thin and pliable and can be flexed to fit the container, while the wood of lattice trellis is fixed in position and may need cutting to shape. Both require securing to upright supports and the whole structure fitted into place before the climber is planted. When in position, secure shoots of the climber to the structure to encourage it to ramble up the support.

As climbers differ in the ways they clamber, choose an appropriate support, such as trellis for this twining clematis.

CLIMBER SUPPORTS

Most climbers require support to enable them to climb. The style and type required will be determined by what type of climber is being grown and your practical and stylistic ambitions for the plant. Potted climbers can be positioned adjacent to a wall and the climbing structure of timber slats,

trellis or wires directly secured to this. Twining plants can be encouraged to cling to the structures, while scrambling plants should be tied in. Plants such as ivies (Hedera) and Virginia creeper (Parthenocissus) are self-clinging and will not require support on a wall, but will if freestanding.

Bind three or more bamboo canes together with garden twine, to form a teepee.

Insert prunings (peasticks) from dormant trees or shrubs among small plants.

Create a cage of galvanized or plastic-coated mesh, supported by bamboo canes.

Position ready-made, galvanized or coated spirals next to each young climber.

Selecting the right growing medium in which to cultivate plants is very important. All container plants need a potting compost that maintains healthy root growth, holds an appropriate amount of moisture and nutrients, provides anchorage for roots and sustains growth for at least a year.

Garden soil is not suitable for containers. While it may support plants adequately in the open garden, issues such as lack of structure, poor drainage and lack of nutrients cause serious

Peat-free composts are manufactured from products such as composted greenwaste and wood fibre.

problems when garden soil is confined to a container. As it is not sterile, the soil can quickly turn sour, leading to the rapid development of toxic conditions, outbreaks of soilborne pests and diseases and germination of weeds.

MULTIPURPOSE POTTING COMPOSTS

For seasonal bedding or where fast, lush growth is required, use a multipurpose potting compost rather than a loam-based one (see box on p137). Multipurpose composts are not ideally suited for seed raising; choose a special seed-sowing mixture instead. When growing lime-hating plants use ericaceous compost. There are also potting composts specially formulated for alpines, cacti and succulents and orchids.

Until recently the most popular multipurpose potting composts were made from decayed sphagnum peat from upland and lowland bogs. Its usefulness stems from the fact it is inert, largely sterile, holds nutrients well and is light in weight. The quality of sphagnum peat is generally consistent, and it was until recently considered almost inexhaustible. In the last decade environmental lobby groups and

LOAM-BASED POTTING COMPOSTS

These are particularly useful for longer-term plantings of trees, shrubs and palms, as the clay content of the loam holds nutrients well and does not decay. Loam-based composts tend not to encourage the rapid, lush growth that many other peat-free composts do. Their extra weight also provides stability for tall plants, so they are not blown over. Britain's John Innes Centre developed a standardised recipe for loam-based potting composts. The JI series is coded 1–3, each increasing in fertiliser content: No 1 is for establishing young plants; No 2 for potting on; and No 3 for longer-term plantings. There is also an ericaceous mix for lime-intolerant plants.

government concern about the impact of peat stripping on the ecology of upland bogs have been the catalyst for the gardening industry to find alternatives to peat, the aim being for all general potting composts for amateurs to be completely peat free by 2020.

Low-peat mixes

The first step has been to reduce the volume of peat blended in potting composts, creating the so-called low-peat mixes. Alternatives, such as composted greenwaste from domestic sources, pulverised wood fibre, shredded pine bark and loam, are variously blended into the mixture.

Peat-free composts

Manufacturers are now striving to produce completely peat-free mixes to achieve government targets. The two foremost candidates used are composted greenwaste and pulverised pinewood. Other smaller and often local producers offer potting mixtures based

on composted straw, bracken fern and sheep wool, among other ingredients.

Composted greenwaste is created from finely chopped garden refuse, mixed with cardboard and paper. This mixture is fast composted and includes various other ingredients. After initial problems caused by the variable nature of raw materials, manufacturers are now achieving a more consistent quality. Greenwaste composts perform differently to peat-based ones, in that they hold nutrients less well and tend to dry more quickly.

The other main type of peat-free compost is based on pulverised wood

Composts for succulents or alpines benefit from additions of grit or perlite to safeguard against waterlogged roots.

fibre. The raw material is produced from conifer wood pulp blasted into small flakes under very high pressure. When mixed with other ingredients, this lightweight potting compost holds nutrients and moisture well and is an effective alternative to peat.

POTTING COMPOST ADDITIVES

Periodically you may need to add materials to potting composts, to improve their drainage or enhance water retention for those plants that particularly require it. Before doing so, always read the manufacturer's instructions about the content and use of the composts. Never add fast-release fertilisers to fresh compost as manufacturers include enough to support the plant for the first few weeks.

Sand & grit

Sands and grits are widely used to improve drainage and aerate the potting compost. They also add weight or bulk and so are ideal for providing ballast to stabilize a containerised shrub or tree. Always use horticultural sand for mixing into composts, because builders' sand is too fine and contains lime, which is detrimental to intolerant plants.

Grit will also add weight and bulk to potting compost, as well as helping improve drainage. Again always use a horticultural-grade product, washed to remove lime and other impurities. Do not add more than equal amounts of grit or sand to the compost.

Perlite

Perlite is a light, crumbly, white granule formed from a mineral. Available in fine or coarse grades, it is mixed into potting composts to improve drainage and provide aeration. It is also useful for adding to composts when rooting cuttings and sowing seeds.

Vermiculite

Vermiculite is created from a mineral called mica. It is light, highly water absorbent and holds nutrients well. It is available in fine or coarse grades and is useful for mixing in composts to improve drainage and water retention. Like perlite, it is particularly effective in plant propagation when rooting cuttings and seed sowing.

WATER-ABSORBING GELS

These are commercially available granules that absorb many hundred times their own weight in water and are added to potting compost to improve the supply of water to the plant. Water is absorbed into the gel from the compost; when the compost dries, the water is still available to the plant via its roots, which grow into the gel. Gels are usually active for 2 years, breaking down after 5. Do not overdose with gel. Check that container and hanging-basket composts do not already contain it.

· ESSENTIAL DRAINAGE ·

The structure of potting compost is important so roots can work efficiently. They provide a plant with support and anchorage as well as a system for obtaining and transporting water and nutrients. Roots also need air, specifically oxygen to respire, thereby releasing carbon dioxide and other waste products into the soil spaces.

If potting compost is too dense, compacted or waterlogged and the volume of air severely reduced, then these dangerous gases will build up to toxic levels to the point that roots stop functioning, become damaged and eventually die. There therefore needs to

be a balance between both moisture and air in the compost, and so its drainage is key in this.

OPTIMISING DRAINAGE

When filling your containers and working soil around the roots, firm to fill empty pockets but do not ram the compost into place to produce airless conditions. Watering the container will help settle compost more efficiently; use a rose attachment.

Placing plants in overlarge pots so they sit in volumes of wet compost is likely to check root and plant development, particularly in cold conditions.

WATERLOGGING

Raising large containers off the ground with proprietary pot feet, stout tiles or bricks will prevent blockages occurring from soil, often aggravated by earthworm activity. It will also help prevent pots from becoming waterlogged by standing water after heavy rain or snow melt. Waterlogging is particularly dangerous for long-term plantings of trees and shrubs, the roots of which are susceptible to being damaged by prolonged contact with water while dormant in winter.

Conversely, massing too many large plants in too small a container enhances drying out, so the compost will require constant watering.

CONTAINER EFFECTS
The type and structure of the container also controls the health of the root environment. Plain terracotta is minutely porous, allowing water to evaporate and potting compost to dry out more quickly than would be the case in impervious, glazed or plastic containers. The shape of the pot also influences how water flows down the sides of the container and how it is directed to the drainage hole. The number and configuration of drainage holes in turn affects how quickly and easily water is discharged from the container.

It is essential there are sufficient drainage holes in the bottom of any plant container. Cheap plastic pots sometimes have drainage holes marked, but not cut out. Clear these completely with a sharp knife.

141

Lightly firming compost around the rootball anchors the plant more securely and improves conditions for new roots.

Drainage holes can become blocked by compost from within or by a soil plug if the pot is placed on the ground. Help keep them open by covering the hole with a curved shard from a broken terracotta pot or roof tile. Adding 2.5–7.5cm (1–3in) layer of coarse pebbles to the bottom of the pot will also help water drain away.

• WATERING PLANTS •

All plants in containers need watering, and it is an important part of your daily routine. Moisture sustains plants and without it they eventually languish and die, unless adapted to drought conditions. Periodic drought also causes flowers to abort or finish quickly. Fruit can also be shed, be disappointing to eat or produce low yields. Plants under stress are also more prone to attack by pests and diseases, such as red spider mite (see p173) and powdery mildew (see p176).

VARIED REQUIREMENTS

The amount of water required will be determined by the number and types of plants being grown, the size and type of pot, its location and the time of year. Succulent or drought-tolerant plants require less frequent watering than large, leafy ornamentals and vegetables, especially fruit crops, such as tomatoes. Small pots dry out much more quickly than larger ones, while porous containers, such as unglazed terracotta, lose more water than plastic or glazed types. Container plants placed in sun use more water than those in shade.

DAILY ROUTINE

Check containers regularly to see if the compost is moist. In large containers, feel around the pot, as some areas may dry out more readily than others. The surface also dries out more quickly, and so surface-rooting or edging plants can be quickly deprived of moisture. Check beneath, as many peat-free composts may look dry, but are often damp below.

LEFT *Small pots require very frequent watering, especially in sun, so use water-absorbing gels to help retain moisture.*

OPPOSITE *Metal containers heat up quickly in sun, and the resulting high temperatures damage plant roots, especially if dry.*

WATERING TECHNIQUES

Mature plantings will require watering daily, or even twice a day in hot or windy conditions. Water early in the morning and/or in the evening, when plants are less stressed. In groups of pots, water small dry plants individually, rather

Pebbles placed on the surface of the pot helps conserve moisture and also adds weight to provide greater stability.

than drenching the whole display. If plants wilt in full sun, move them to a shady spot while they recover. Water the compost using a watering can or hosepipe; allow sufficient time for the water to soak in before watering again. To reach elevated containers, try an extendable lance (see box on p34).

If plants in small pots have completely dried out, plunge them into a bucket of water. Adding a drop or two of washing-up liquid to the water will help dry compost remoisten more readily.

Ensure drainage holes do not become blocked, causing waterlogging and wilting of plants (see p177).

AUTOMATIC IRRIGATION

Automated or micro-irrigation watering systems come in a variety of designs, usually supplied as hosepipe attachments. With careful installation and experience they can significantly reduce the burden of watering. Micro-irrigation systems enable more localised application of water via small sprays, jets or drips and can be located and adjusted to deliver water in particular ways to specific plants. They can also be used to apply liquid feed, but may need to be flushed out occasionally to prevent build-ups of feed encrustations from blocking nozzles.

Also useful are seep hoses. These lengths of porous rubber or plastic pipe

Irrigation systems enable plants to be watered just by turning on the tap. They need installing with care to be effective.

are laid on the surface or buried in the container, which gently and gradually allows moisture to percolate into the compost, watering all the plants at once.

HOLIDAY PLANT CARE

Ensuring plants are kept watered while you are away can be a problem. For a day or so, use one of the many systems available with small reservoir tanks or bags of water fitted to drip irrigation nozzles. If absent for extended lengths of time, it might be worth investing in a programmable switch system, which connects to your mains water supply. When linked into a micro-irrigation network, this will deliver water at predetermined times of day. Alternatively, use more drought-tolerant plants.

145

• FEEDING PLANTS •

All plants in containers require feeding to stimulate growth and help produce flowers and/or fruit. Most growing media contain fertilisers that will sustain plants from a few weeks to a few months. However, many plants benefit from supplementary feeding, usually applied in liquid form.

NUTRIENTS IN FERTILISER

All fertilisers are labelled to show their nutrient content in terms of nitrogen (N), phosphorus (P) and potassium (K); they may also include traces of other elements in much smaller quantities. Nitrogen stimulates stem and leaf growth and phosphorus aids root development while potassium (potash) encourages flowers and fruit.

While in growth, plants require a balance of these nutrients, and in different amounts at various times of the year, depending on what the plant is doing. While plants are immature, they require more nitrogen, but once in flower and forming fruit they benefit from higher dosages of potassium.

FERTILISER TYPES

Fertilisers are also available in granular, pelleted and liquid form. There are fast- and slow-release fertilisers as well as a blend of both types.

Always read the manufacturer's instructions about each product before using it, so you can ensure that you have the appropriate fertiliser and that you are applying it correctly. By using too much or the wrong kind of fertiliser you can seriously affect performance and even damage plants. Water all fertilisers in well, particularly if the weather is dry.

Granular & pelleted fertilisers

Permanent plantings, such as trees, shrubs or palms, will benefit from an application of a granular fertiliser worked into the top centimetre or so of the potting compost just before growth starts; this is known as topdressing. Use a balanced general-purpose type (such as growmore or blood, fish and bone) or pelleted chicken manure, which is high in nitrogen. Acid-loving or ericaceous plants (such as rhododendron) and specialist plants (such as orchids, cacti and succulents) require particular types of fertiliser that are most appropriate for their needs.

Pellets of fertiliser can be pushed into rootballs of mature potted plants to feed roots directly.

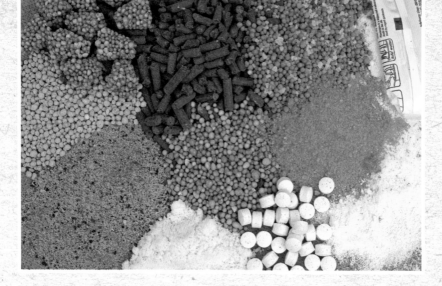

Liquid feeds

Liquid fertiliser is the easiest way to feed container plants, because it can be applied directly as little and as often as required. Feeds vary from those with a balanced NPK (suitable for general use) to those high in potassium (used for fruit crops, such as tomatoes and flowering ornamentals). There are also liquid fertilisers suitable for ericaceous plants and others, such as for orchids or succulents.

Liquid feed concentrates are diluted in water at the rate recommended by the manufacturer. Most are applied once a week or every two weeks, depending

Fertiliser blends, types and methods of application vary, so match the needs of your plants to the appropriate fertiliser. Always read manufacturer's instructions on dosage levels, and on how and when the product should be applied.

on the type of plant and circumstances. Most liquid fertilisers are applied by watering can or by a diluter fixed to a tap, which introduces feed concentrate into flowing water.

Always ensure the rootball is moist before applying liquid fertiliser; avoid giving it to dry or wilted plants. Allow wilted plants to recover, then feed them.

• POTTING ON & REPLANTING •

Perennials, particularly woody ones, require potting on as they grow larger and as their roots fill their containers. As they become increasingly constrained in their search for moisture and nutrients, becoming what is known as root-bound, plants will need watering and feeding far more frequently. If such supplies are curtailed or intermittent, this results in poor growth and performance, stunting or die-back of shoots. This said, a minority of fleshy-rooted perennials, such as African lily (*Agapanthus*), seem to flower more productively if allowed to become root-bound.

POTTING ON

While they are small and young, plants can be transferred into progressively larger pots with relative ease. Pots should usually be 10–20cm (4–8in) wider and 5–10cm (2–4in) deeper than previously; give woody plants slightly more (see p132).

Never place small plants in overlarge containers, because they can struggle to re-establish themselves when surrounded by so much compost.

Try to remain consistent in the type of potting compost used when repotting; never alternate between multipurpose and loam-based types.

Ensure you have all the elements to hand before planting. Pot the plant in its final site if the finished container will be heavy.

Find out which type of compost your plant prefers and avoid alternating between different types when repotting.

REPLANTING

When a plant gets too big to transfer to a larger container, you can retain it in its current pot provided you scrape off some of the old compost from the rootball and replace it with fresh. This technique is particularly useful when growing trees and large shrubs, such as maples (*Acer*), sweet bay (*Laurus nobilis*), box (*Buxus*) or yew (*Taxus*). Roots can also be shortened to help control growth.

149

POTTING ON INTO A LARGER CONTAINER

Moisten the rootball before transferring a plant to a larger container once its roots have filled the existing pot. For small plants, choose a pot that is 5–7.5cm (2–3in) wider than the previous one.

Carefully slip the stem between two fingers and, while supporting the rootball, invert and tap the pot edge against a bench edge to loosen the pot. Plastic pots are easier to remove than terracotta ones.

Fill the bottom of the new pot with potting compost so the top of the rootball sits 2cm (³/₄in) below the rim, to allow for watering. Add more compost around the rootball and firm lightly. Water in the plant.

• SUPPORT IN POTS •

Many plants either need or benefit from being supported when grown in pots. The amount and type of support required is determined by the plant type. Climbers with twining or scrambling shoots or shrubs with lax growth always require support, but other tall or slender-stemmed plants may also benefit from being held in position to help prevent them collapsing, particularly if exposed to strong wind or heavy rain. Supports of increasing strength and durability will be required as plants grow older, taller and heavier – even with annuals.

Supports add character to plantings just as much as the pot, but ensure they meet the practical needs of the plant.

NATURAL SUPPORT

Supports come in many different forms – from the subtle to the strongly architectural – and often make a statement in themselves. However, unless the latter is the objective, always choose a system that provides unobtrusive support for best results. Twigs and brushwood prunings from deciduous trees and shrubs are particularly effective for thin-stemmed and twining climbers. These can be pruned to create interesting shapes for such plants to grow over; they can also be tied together to provide natural-looking supports for herbaceous plants. If you can't source any twigs and brushwood yourself, look for local suppliers of woodland thinnings.

Slender climbers, such as sweet peas (*Lathyrus odoratus*) or smaller clematis, can also be grown over the framework of larger shrubs. Bamboo canes, which come in a range of sizes, can similarly be used; secure the stems with loops of twine. Canes can also be made into wigwams between plants or around the edges of a container. Weave twine in and around the plant stems to produce cradles or webs of support.

ARCHITECTURAL STYLES

Woven structures of willow (*Salix*), such as obelisks or teepees, are ideal for supporting more robust climbers, but their shape does not allow anything to be grown other than around the edge of the pot. Alternatively, create your own style by weaving lengths of willow stems into interesting shapes.

Supports are also available from folded metal hoops or rods to moulded plastic, from simple to highly ornate (see also box on p135). Also discarded household and garden objects can be recycled to provide impromptu and often quirky support structures.

SECURING GROWTH

When securing stems, remember that jute twine will decay after a matter of months, while polypropylene string lasts almost indefinitely.

Twiggy growth, known as peasticks, can be added to provide unobtrusive support to short plants.

Therefore, always use the latter in long-term plantings. You can also obtain a wide variety of plastic clips – galvanized, plastic or foam-coated wire – which will not chafe shoots and are useful for a variety of situations. Leave the tie slightly loose against the support, to allow stems to expand. Check regularly that growth does not become garrotted in longer-term plantings.

• WIND & FROST PROTECTION •

Perennials and woody plants often need protection against winter weather in cool-temperate regions, particularly in exposed positions. Wind and frost are damaging in themselves, but they are far more deadly in combination, because very low air temperatures suck moisture from leaves. Evergreen trees, shrubs and conifers are susceptible, as moisture stripped from foliage cannot be replaced from frozen rootballs, thus causing scorched foliage.

SHELTERED ACCOMMODATION

If possible, move susceptible container plantings to a sheltered position before the first frosts, especially if borderline hardy. Ideally, plants at risk from frost damage are best overwintered in a glasshouse or conservatory, which is heated to remain frost-free.

Many plants, but particularly cacti, succulents and tender bulbs, will tolerate lower air temperatures provided their roots are kept dry or just moist, so damaging frost is not able to penetrate. Bulbs such as Indian shot plant (*Canna*) and dahlias can also be lifted, top growth and compost removed and then be stored dry in a frost-free garage or shed. Check the health of plants regularly.

OUTDOOR PROTECTION

The combination of winter wet and freezing conditions is a killer for certain plants while dormant, such as some alpines or bulbs subjected to damp winters that constantly freeze and thaw. If grown outdoors, protect these plants with a shelter constructed from a sheet of glass, Perspex or polythene so it sheds water and thereby protects the plant.

Other plants can be protected from the elements in winter by using a range of products such as the following.

Horticultural fleece

A sheet or number of sheets of fleece draped over a plant or made into a tent will afford significant protection against drying winds, winter wet and hard frost. It also allows air to move and light to penetrate. Use it to protect tender spring growth against late frosts.

Hessian sacking

This also makes a good shelter and will protect plants against heavy snow and frost but, being heavier than fleece, it needs support. Hessian is useful for wrapping stems of trees and shrubs, but not for covering evergreen foliage as it does not allow sufficient light through

Wrap sheets of horticultural fleece, bubble wrap or sacking around bamboo canes inserted well into the potting compost in the container; secure in place with polypropylene string.

Work straw or dry bracken around plant leaves and stems and encase with plastic mesh or chicken wire screwed to the wall with fixings.

Provide temporary cover against hard frost or snow by covering plants at risk with a stout hessian sack.

To protect a plant and its roots, plunge the pot into the ground up to its rim. Pack a straw or bracken mulch around the stems and leaves and wrap them with horticultural fleece or bubble wrap.

153

for growth. When secured to posts, it is useful for creating a protective screen to slow damaging winds.

Straw cages

Dry straw is an effective insulator, and susceptible plants or even whole plantings can be protected by creating a cage of wire mesh and packing the space around the plants with loose straw. This is especially effective for protecting the stems and growing points of tree ferns, palms and banana (*Musa*) plants.

Plunging pots

Winter temperatures below ground are a few degrees higher than those of the air and so plunging pots of some plants below ground level will afford some protection. This technique is particularly helpful for those plants of borderline hardiness that can regenerate from roots, such as fuchsia, or for bulbs, corms or tubers. Cover the surface of the pot with a mulch of straw or bark chips and secure in position, or wrap up plunged plants (see box above).

• DECORATIVE DETAILS •

New containers always stand out from their surroundings, but the effects of weather soon start to age the material so it harmonises with the garden and loses its shiny newness.

AGING GRACEFULLY

Untreated (but not glazed) terracotta, concrete and reconstituted or natural stone mellow beautifully. This is due not only to sunlight but also to moisture held in their finely porous structures, which enables microscopic, simple

plants, such as algae, lichens and mosses, to colonise these materials.

AGELESS SOLUTIONS

If you don't want your containers to mellow, choose pots made from plastics or resins, which are often realistically modelled to give the patina of decay. Pots metallised with chrome or made of metal covered with a clear sealant are weather-resistant and retain much of their raw, bright tone.

METAL TONES

Other metals age by often forming a thin veneer of oxide as they slowly react with the elements. Aluminium and lead go dull silver or white; copper, a blue-green called verdigris; and iron turns to the red-orange dust known as rust. These coatings can be removed by cleaning or coating the metal with a clear sealant.

ATTRACTIVE SURFACINGS

Decorative mulches are usually applied to longer-term plantings, such as trees, shrubs, alpines, cacti and succulents. These coverings on pot surfaces act as a barrier, deterring weeds, mosses or liverworts from colonising the potting compost beneath them. Dressings also

NEW BECOMES OLD

Speed the aging process by encouraging algae and mosses to colonise the surfaces of your pots. Evenly paint or dab the exterior and rim of a container with milk, or else use a solution of natural yogurt watered into a runny paste, adding a teaspoon of honey or sugar per cup of yogurt. You can also pulverise a few common moss plants and add them to the mixture. Such a mixture looks messy, but will soon disappear and algae will start to flourish. Alternatively purchase proprietary products that perform the same task.

help prevent moisture loss and keep roots cool. Most materials can be used as a decorative mulch as long as they are:

● Porous, allowing water to pass to the compost below.

● Inert, that is, not harmful to plants or likely to contaminate the compost: for example, use alkaline limestone chips on lime-lovers – never on plants preferring acid soils, such as rhododendron.

To be effective, decorative mulches need to be 2.5–5cm (1–2in) thick. The main disadvantages of such topdressing are that it is more difficult to gauge when plants require watering and when adding granular fertilisers.

Before applying a decorative mulch to an established, container-grown plant, always skim off the surface of the compost and remove the roots of all perennial, taprooted weeds.

When worked around the neck of plants that like free-draining soil, such as alpines or succulents, decorative mulches, such as grits or gravels, aid drainage and prevent damp conditions, which can encourage rots, particularly in winter.

The shards of terracotta covering the surface of these raised beds help keep down weeds and retain moisture.

Weighty topdressings can also be used to help anchor tall plants in containers or make them less liable to being blown over by strong winds.

VISUAL EFFECT

Topdressings provide a clean foil against which to display plants to best effect. Natural or subtle tones complement plants better than bright colours, while coloured gravels, metallised pebbles and glass chips can make a bold statement.

• MOVING CONTAINERS •

The beauty of containers is that they can be positioned wherever they are required. Small pots can be easily grouped and relocated on a whim. However, large containers, such as half-barrels and urns laden with plants and damp compost, are far too heavy to move without employing significant effort and equipment. It therefore makes sense to plant up such containers *in situ*, rather than move them into position later.

SAFE PRACTICE

Get someone to help you lift and support a large container, and then use a sack-barrow or low-wheeled trolley to transport it. It may help to start by raising the pot off the floor with pot feet or bricks, so the lip of the trolley can get beneath it. Unwieldy empty urns or barrels can also be transported by wheelbarrow. To fill the barrow, hold it upright and then gradually slide the edge of the pot onto the front lip of the barrow. Tilt back the barrow and slide the urn into the pan (see box below). Never move very heavy objects without lifting safely and within your capability.

MOBILE CONTAINERS

There are various wheeled platforms available on which to place pots, so they can be moved around hard surfaces. The more even and smooth the surface, the better they work. On sloping ground they will need chocking in place.

PROBLEMS DURING TRANSIT

Always take care when transporting fragile containers, such as terracotta ones, as dropping them even a centimetre or bumping edges on hard surfaces can crack them. Wooden barrels will often start to fall apart when moved, as the metal hoops slip off. Either spray the barrels to moisten and re-expand the wood, or else tack the hoops in place.

Make lifting and moving containers easier by choosing ones with handles, or place them on a wheeled platform.

MOVING HEAVY POTS

To move a heavy container, place a wheelbarrow on end and tip the pot into the barrow pan. Tilt the pan slowly back until it is horizontal, fully supporting the bulk and weight of the pot as you do so.

Effective container displays are always composed of healthy plants kept in tiptop condition. As well as watering and feeding, this means ensuring plants are tidy by routinely picking them over, removing spent flowers, flowerheads and dead or dying leaves.

ROUTINE TASKS

It is best to do these jobs little and often, perhaps taking a few minutes as you pass by, so plants have to make only small growth adjustments, rather than a more substantial recovery from the impact of one intensive session. Not only does this improve their visual presentation but also, by removing spent flowers and flowerheads of many bedding plants, you often stimulate more to form and you curtail the plant's tendency to start setting seed. Sweet peas (*Lathyrus odoratus*) are a case in point: their display of flowers is dramatically shortened if withered blossoms are not quickly harvested.

DEALING WITH FOLIAGE

As plants grow and develop, their lower leaves become shaded, and being surplus to requirements often wither away; they should be removed. Overcongested foliage of mature bedding plants can also be thinned out, allowing more air to penetrate, helping prevent attacks by fungal diseases, such as grey mould. If you prefer not to use pesticides to control pests and diseases, such as red spider mite (see p173) or powdery mildew (see p176), picking off affected leaves as soon as outbreaks are spotted will also help control their spread.

KEEPING PLANTS NEAT

Prune away unwanted, thin or unruly growth from climbers after flowering and secure the remainder of the shoots to a support or stout framework.

Remove spent flowerheads to encourage others to form and to prevent plants wasting their energy by producing seed that is not required.

REVIVING BEDDING

As the season progresses, bedding plants will eventually start to falter. If not being replaced with new bedding, many 'old troopers', such as diascia, scaevola, violets (*Viola*) and pinks (*Dianthus*), can be given a new lease of life by being cut back with shears. Snip off the stems 5–7.5cm (2–3in) above the ground, then water and apply liquid feed. After a week or two, new growth should have emerged to refresh the display with foliage and flowers, although the second flush of blossoms is not likely to be as intense as the first.

Make picking over plants to remove spent foliage and flowers part of your routine to keep them looking their best.

SPRING CLEANING

Architectural perennials, such as the grasses miscanthus and molinia, often provide autumn colour when left to catch the frost, alongside late flowering perennials, such as coneflower (*Rudbeckia*). All these can be cut back hard in late winter or spring, just before growth commences. Tussock-forming grasses, such as fescues (*Festuca*), also benefit from having old leaves teased out with a tined cultivator or hand rake.

CHELSEA CHOP

Many perennials benefit from having their flowers and straggly foliage cut off in early summer, to encourage new growth – the so-called 'Chelsea chop'. Being cut back in this way suits some late spring-flowering plants, such as cranesbill (*Geranium*) and lady's mantle (*Alchemilla mollis*). Other perennials, such as coral flower (*Heuchera*), can also look bedraggled after winter and benefit from being sheared in spring, just before the new growth starts.

• PRUNING PLANTS •

All woody plants in containers, whether trees, shrubs or climbers, require pruning every so often, to remove dead or dying shoots, control and shape growth, and help influence flowering. When pruning, always use a pair of sharp secateurs or shears to secure a clean cut.

PRUNING FOR HEALTH

Shoots on woody plants often die back. This occurs for many reasons, such as frost damage from harsh winters (particularly with evergreens) and from prolonged drought or poor growing conditions in summer.

Dead growth needs to be removed to prevent infection by fungal diseases as well as to improve visual quality. These can seriously damage plants, so inspect them regularly, and treat as required (see p171). Where possible, always cut about 2.5cm (1in) below the dead portion, into healthy green growth or where new shoots are sprouting. Dispose of or burn all dead or diseased material, rather than composting it.

TOPIARY

Shrubs and trees, particularly evergreens such as box (*Buxus*), sweet bay (*Laurus nobilis*), yew (*Taxus*) and many other conifers, can be pruned to create formal and informal shapes, collectively known as topiary. This technique continues to be as popular today as in history.

Evergreens, such as box and yew, can be trimmed into topiary shapes. Do this in spring or autumn for optimal results.

Formal topiary involves pinching, clipping and training shoots to produce geometric shapes, such as pyramids, spheres, cubes or artifacts. It can be created by placing a shaped metal form over a shrub or tree and then pruning growth to the required shape over successive seasons. These shapes can also be created on a standard tree, with the shaped canopy above the main stem or trunk cleared of branches and foliage.

Informal clipping and training of a tree or shrub allows you to shape foliage to various artistic forms, such as 'clouds', as in the Japanese art of cloud pruning.

FRUIT TREE SHAPES

Fruit trees can also be pruned to achieve a particular shape, such as an espalier, fan or cordon. This will enhance tree productivity, and so optimum yields can be achieved in a small space.

ROOT PRUNING

The periodic pruning away of a number of larger roots on woody plants can help control growth of the plant, prevent roots from spiralling around the pot and stimulate new roots to form. This is one of the ways in which bonsai trees are kept dwarf and undertaken when

dormant. If unsure about doing this seek further advice before starting.

PRUNING & FLOWERING

Many woody plants, particularly shrubs, are grown especially for their flowers. While they will blossom without human interference, the flowering of many is enhanced by pruning growth in the right way at the right time. When this is done depends on their flowering season.

● Hardy shrubs flowering in spring to early summer do so on growth made the previous year. Therefore, prune off flowerheads and shoots immediately after blossoming, cutting back to fresh, new growth.

● Hardy shrubs flowering in summer and autumn usually do so on growth made the same year, so prune back old growth in early spring to the base or to a suitably sized framework from where new flowering growth will form.

Some tender, subtropical, woody plants, such as blue potato bush (*Lycianthes rantonnettii*), may flower all year round and so require pruning only to keep them in bounds and to shape.

• BASKET BASICS •

Success with suspended plantings depends on a number of factors, such as the size of the container, the nature and quality of the plantings, and most importantly how well you look after them. As they are often located in exposed positions, hanging baskets are apt to dry out more quickly than pots on the ground – smaller baskets far more quickly than larger ones (see p34). Being raised above eye level also makes it more difficult to keep a check on moisture levels in the potting compost. Thankfully, there are a number of

products and techniques that help make caring for baskets that much easier, leaving you more time to enjoy the floral show.

BASKET TYPES

Hanging baskets come in a wide variety of shapes and sizes, which require different approaches to the way they are managed. Look at where they are to be located to help select the best option.

Woven mesh

The mesh allows the sides of the basket to be planted up by threading small plantlets through the gaps, so ensure the gaps are wide enough to enable you to do this.

   Traditional are the hemispherical, open-weave, galvanized mesh baskets, but hanging baskets are also made from plastic mesh or woven willow. All require lining and an impervious reservoir placed in the bottom to stop water running straight through. Plastic or willow types may already have these facilities in place.

A well-planted hanging basket demands to be displayed to best effect, but always ensure it is securely supported.

Moulded plastic

Solid bowls, or baskets, usually moulded from plastic, retain moisture for longer. Check there are sufficient drainage holes punctured in the base to allow excess moisture to escape.

Some models have dishes attached to the base to act as reservoirs, which can lead to waterlogging in consistently wet weather. Look for those that are detachable. Other models have integral reservoir systems moulded into the base, supplying water by means of capilliary wicks, again helping cut down on manual watering.

BASKET LINERS

Mesh baskets are traditionally lined with live sphagnum or woodland moss, but this practice is now not encouraged because of concerns about damaging their habitat and the need for conservation. Instead, you can use moss raked from lawns or moss taken from elsewhere in your own garden.

Manufactured liners

Instead of moss you can use manufactured liners to act as a barrier for mesh or open-weave baskets to help retain compost and hold in moisture. Such liners are usually circular and

The perforated polythene liner in this mesh basket retains moisture in the soil without waterlogging it.

cut into thin wedges from the centre rather like a pizza, allowing them to be moulded to a variety of basket shapes (see box on p33). They can be made from jute, synthetic matting, coir fibre or perforated polythene.

These liners make it more difficult to locate plants in the side of the basket, except in gaps where the liners have already been cut. Thinner liners of polythene can be slit with a sharp knife, whereas thick coir liners are much tougher to cut.

You will be able to plant through the sides of a hanging basket if you perforate its liner with a sharp knife.

Recycled liners

You can make your own liners using perforated polythene sheeting, mulching fabric or old cloths. Place a tin pie tray, tin foil or polythene sheeting in the centre to act as a water reservoir. You could also experiment using large, tough evergreen leaves, such as *Fatsia* or hardy palms.

BASKET PLANTS

Plants suitable for hanging baskets are many and varied (see box on p165). The effects created will depend not only on the basket type, but also on practical issues, such as the width and volume of the basket, whether you can plant up the side, how heavy it will be and where it will be hung (see p34). Plants will often be buffeted by strong wind and subjected to intense sunlight so your plants will need to withstand these conditions.

Although hanging baskets are seen as items for summer display, they can also be used for other seasonal bedding, particularly in late winter or spring or contain plantings of dwarf shrubs, compact perennials, bulbs or alpines. They are also good for dwarf fruit and vegetables as well as herbs.

PLANTS FOR HANGING BASKETS

ORNAMENTALS

Feature plants

Fuchsia

Heliotropium (heliotrope)

Impatiens (busy Lizzie)

Nemesia

Osteospermum

Pelargonium (geranium)

Petunia

Salvia farinacea, *S. splendens*

Solenostemon (coleus)

Succulents, such as *Crassula*, *Echeveria*, *Pachyphytum* and *Sedum* (stonecrop)

Edging & side of basket plants

Begonia hybrids from *B. boliviensis*

Calibrachoa

Campanula isophylla (star-of-Bethlehem)

Dichondra micrantha

Hedera helix (English ivy) cultivars

Lobelia

Pelargonium peltatum

Sutera

Verbena

Viola (violet), *V.* × *wittrockiana* (pansy)

Herbs

Allium schoenoprasum (chives)

Coriandrum (coriander)

Helichrysum italicum

Lavandula (lavender)

Ocimum basilicum (basil)

Origanum (marjoram), *O. vulgare* (oregano)

Petroselinum (parsley)

Salvia (sage)

Thymus (thyme)

Vegetables

Beetroot

Chilli pepper and dwarf sweet pepper

Cut-and-come-again salad

Dwarf small-fruited cucumber

Dwarf cherry tomato

Dwarf French bean

Dwarf lettuce

Landcress

Peas and mangetout

Radish

Spring onion

Soft fruit

Fragaria (strawberry), including *F. vesca* (alpine strawberry)

Rubus articus (Arctic raspberry)

Vaccinium (cranberry)

Strawberries make ideal plants for a dual-purpose hanging basket.

• PLANTING HANGING BASKETS •

The work involved in putting together a hanging basket all depends on the type of basket you choose. Simplest is a solid, plastic bowl, or basket, where you need to plant up only the top. A little more complicated is a mesh basket, in which you can also plant up the sides.

Given the weight of a fully planted hanging basket requiring support, use lightweight, peat-free, multipurpose potting compost, rather than a loam-based one. Many peat-free blends are specially formulated for baskets and containers and have a water-absorbent gel mixed in. If not, purchase the gel separately and mix it in yourself.

SOLID BOWLS

Ensure the plants are well watered. Fill the bottom of the basket with potting compost and then set out the plants. Depending on container size, plant the largest in the centre, then the supporting plants and finish with edging or cascading plants around the rim. Once in place, pack plenty of compost around each rootball. Water the hanging basket

Coir liners are made from coated palm husk fibre. Being thick and durable, they are difficult to cut to plant up basket sides.

in well and allow to drain. Rather than hanging up the basket straight away, it helps to settle the plants if they can have a few days in the protected conditions of a glasshouse or conservatory while they make new root and shoot growth.

MESH BASKETS

When planting, it is important to support the hanging basket on the rim of a stout, plastic pot or bucket.

Fitting the liner

If using recycled moss from a lawn as a basket liner (see p163), moisten and work a layer 1–2.5cm (½–1in) thick over the inner surface, ensuring there are no gaps; then place a small pie tin or circle of foil or polythene in the base as a water reservoir (see p33). Alternatively,

PLANTING A HANGING BASKET USING A MOSS LINER

Support the hanging basket with a pot or bucket. Use sphagnum moss from approved sources or some moss from your own lawn to pack the base of the basket. Then insert a plastic disc or pie dish as a reservoir and add potting compost.

On reaching planting height with the potting compost, insert the rootball of a small plug plant or clumps of seedlings through the mesh and moss. Continue inserting plants through the sides and adding compost up to the top of the basket.

Plant the centre of the basket with a feature plant, and surround it with supporting plants, which can cascade over the sides.

When the basket is finished, soak the compost thoroughly to bed in the plants. Place the hanging basket in the glasshouse until the plants have become established, then harden them off and hang the basket outdoors on a secure fitting.

use fabric or similar liners. When using polythene as a basket liner, ensure it is perforated (except in the centre for the reservoir) to allow water to escape. If utilising a manufactured liner, mould this to the inside of the basket, overlapping the flaps to fit.

Inserting the plants

To plant up the sides, fill the basket with potting compost to the level at which the plants are required, then slit the liner with a sharp knife (or push through the moss) and carefully feed the rootball through the slit from the outside of the basket. Pack with compost, leaving the neck of the plant flush with the basket. (Work in more moss around the neck of the plant, if appropriate.) Repeat the process as often as required.

WATERING TECHNIQUES

Unless it has an inbuilt reservoir, a hanging basket can dry out quickly, especially in hot and/or windy weather. It needs to be checked every day and in the height of summer may require watering once or twice a day, especially if baskets are small (see p144).

Make watering easier and more accurate by using an extendable lance and rose on the hosepipe or a rise-and-fall pulley to bring baskets down to a convenient height for watering, feeding and maintaining plants (see box on p34). If a number of baskets are planned, consider setting up a drip irrigation system to each basket (see p145).

Because of the minimal amounts of compost in these shallow containers, nutrients are quickly depleted, so water baskets weekly with a balanced or high-potash liquid fertiliser.

FIXING BASKETS

A fully laden, irrigated hanging basket can be very heavy. To support the weight, fixings need to be strong and secure, or the consequences can be disastrous and potentially dangerous.

Before purchasing, check basket stays are strong and durable enough; the metal chains should preferably be galvanized, and good anchor points are essential.

Brackets should be cast iron or alloy and be substantial enough for the size of basket. They should be secured to masonry or wood by three screws or bolts not less than 10cm (4in) long. Never suspend a hanging basket by string or twine, as its weight may well exceed the breaking strain, especially after natural deterioration.

HANGING BASKET RECIPES

Plan baskets beforehand, whether growing ornamentals or vegetables. Ornamental baskets need a central feature plant, such as a flowering fuchsia, pelargonium, begonia or coleus (*Solenostemon*) for foliage. Surround with pansies (*Viola* × *wittrockiana*), calibrachoa, creeping zinnias (*Sanvitalia*) or petunia. Around the edge or sides plant trailing flowering plants such as lobelia, sutera or verbena. For foliage, use variegated ivies (*Hedera*) and catmint (*Nepeta*), or silvery dichondra.

Vegetables and herbs are attractive and useful. Select dwarf varieties of cherry tomatoes and peppers. Red-leaved 'Bull's Blood' beetroot and 'Lollo Rossa' lettuce add colour. Also try compact herbs such as variegated oregano and basil (*Ocimum*).

Sun-loving herbs are ideal plants with which to create your own practical and useful hanging garden.

• PESTS, DISEASES
& COMMON PROBLEMS •

Most plantings in containers will be affected by problems at some point during the year, whether you grow flowers, fruit or vegetables. Avoid as many of these as possible by ensuring you use good-quality plants and then keep them growing in conditions to which they are most suited. Healthy plants are less likely to develop diseases and are better able to recover from pest infestations.

REGULAR INSPECTIONS

Get into the habit of examining your plants as often as you can, checking leaves are healthy, looking beneath them and in flower buds for any signs of pest infestation or fungal diseases. Pick off dead or dying foliage and avoid planting too densely so that dank, humid conditions build up, which can attract particular fungal diseases. Unless required, remove spent flowers to prevent seeds forming and using up valuable resources.

OPTIMUM CONDITIONS

Fresh air flowing through plants combined with good sunlight will toughen growth and help make it more resistant to damage. Water plants regularly and evenly (see p142); never allow them to wilt constantly as this will both stress and weaken the plant. While feeding will help sustain healthy growth (see p146), avoid overuse of high-nitrogen fertilisers as the soft, sappy growth produced will make plants a target for sucking insects, such as greenfly (see p172).

CLIMATIC EFFECTS

Prevailing weather will favour one or more pests or diseases in different seasons and from year to year. Some plants, such as those in the tomato family (Solanaceae), are particularly prone to attack by particular types of pest, such as red spider mite (see p173) and whitefly (see p175). When growing fruit or vegetables look for cultivars that have been bred for resistance to common potentially devastating diseases, such as mildew (see p176) or blights, or have been bred for conditions local to you, as this will help plants cope and remain productive. Always treat problems as soon as possible.

PESTICIDES & FUNGICIDES

The decision as to whether to use pesticides and other garden chemicals is a matter of personal persuasion. In recent years, the range of pesticides has been drastically reduced for political, social and commercial reasons, and the range of more natural products has been increased to take their place.

Some pesticides are contact ones, that is, they kill the organism that is sprayed. Contact pesticides may remain active (persistent) for a short while after application. Most are now of low persistence, so they may need to be reapplied if problems persist or reoccur.

The other type of pesticide is a systemic one, which is absorbed into the plant, remaining active for some time, killing the pest when it feeds. Fungicides kill on contact with the relevant fungus.

PLANT HYGIENE

As there may be some pest or disease problems for which there is currently no reliable cure for home gardeners, your main means of defence is maintaining good growing conditions or using resistant plants. Be hygienic at all times and keep equipment, growing spaces and pots clean. Always use good-quality materials and sharp tools.

Provide seedlings and young plants with enough space and light, as overcrowding will lead to spindly, weak growth, as here.

171

APHIDS (GREENFLY, BLACKFLY)

These very common, small, sap-sucking, highly mobile insects in shades of green or black are generally located beneath leaves or clustered around shoot tips. Growth often becomes distorted or leaves puckered, and the aphids excrete honeydew, making leaves below sticky and covered in black, sooty mould. Aphids can also spread viral diseases, causing yellow mottling of foliage. Remove aphids by wiping off the insects or use contact insecticides based on plant oils, fatty acids or pyrethrum. For prolonged control, try a systemic pesticide, such as thiacloprid. Some aphids infest roots, so drench with systemic pesticide and wash pots before use.

LILY BEETLES

These very damaging pests from Eurasia, found in mainland Europe and the UK, rapidly defoliate lilies (*Lilium*) and fritillaries (*Fritillaria*). Adults are scarlet, about 8mm ($^{1}/_{3}$in) long, with black heads and legs. Larvae are of similar size but have orange bodies covered in black slime. Orange egg masses are laid on the underside of leaves. Larvae and adults feed on the leaves between spring and autumn. Pick off and destroy adults and larvae as soon as seen. When it is impractical to pick by hand, spray with an insecticide containing thiacloprid or acetamiprid periodically as required.

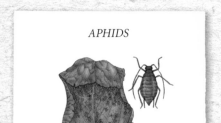

APHIDS

LILY BEETLE

MEALYBUGS

Mealybugs are small, sap-feeding insects hidden under white, waxy fibres, which cause problems in plantings in glasshouses and conservatories. Succulents, grapevines (*Vitis*), citrus plants and other perennial and shrubby glasshouse plants are particularly susceptible. Infected plants become covered in adults and egg masses, and are soiled in honeydew and sooty mould. Roots can also be infested. To control mealybugs, pick off adults and egg masses. Then use the systemic insecticide acetamiprid or thiacloprid on ornamentals, or apply fatty acids and plant oils on grapevines.

RED SPIDER MITES

Minute, orange-red or straw-coloured mites suck sap from lower leaf surfaces, causing leaves to become mottled or speckled with yellow. The presence of fine-silk webbing covered with mites indicates a heavy infestation, which may result in leaf fall. Red spider mites prefer glasshouse conditions and hot, dry, summer weather. Cool or humid conditions keep it in check, so spray plants with water when temperatures rise. If infestation does occur, spray plants with plant oils and fatty acids, thoroughly covering leaf undersides. Ornamental plants can be sprayed with thiamethhoxam or abamectin.

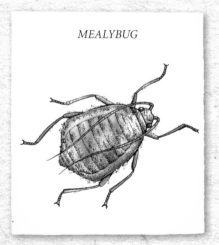

MEALYBUG

RED SPIDER MITE

SCALE INSECTS

Small, soft-bodied, straw-coloured or brown insects, 2–5mm ($^1/_{12}$–$^1/_4$in) long, feed off plant sap. The adults cluster along leaf veins and stems of evergreen perennial and shrubby plants, particularly citrus, sweet bay (*Laurus nobilis*), oleander (*Nerium*) and grapevines (*Vitis*). Some secrete honeydew, making the leaf surface below sticky and covered with sooty mould. Wipe scale insects off the plant as soon as seen, or spray with deltamethrin or thiacloprid, which will be absorbed by the plant. Pesticidal preparations containing fatty acids and plant oils provide some control of young nymphs if symptoms are caught early.

SLUGS & SNAILS

These common pests cause catastrophic damage by consuming young leaves and new shoots on herbaceous plants, such as plantain lilies (*Hosta*), leaving them full of holes. Damage increases in wet weather, when slugs are more active. They hide under pot rims and dark recesses in plantings. Some slug species also live in the soil, where they damage potato tubers and bulbs. Attacks can be controlled by inspecting plants and pot rims, especially moulded plastic ones, at night when slugs are most active. Raise pots off the ground and scatter slug pellets containing metaldehyde or ferric phosphate around the base of plants. Try physical barriers, such as copper tape wound around the pot, or repellent gels.

SCALE INSECTS

SLUGS & SNAILS

VINE WEEVILS

Potted plants are particularly susceptible to these common pests. Both the adult beetles and grubs cause damage to many plants, sometimes terminally. Adult weevils are black, highly mobile insects, 9mm ($^3/_8$in) long, and active at night. They crawl up plant stems and eat notches in leaf margins, particularly evergreen shrubs, such as rhododendron. The larvae are creamy white, brown-headed grubs that feed on the roots of many container plants, particularly corms and bulbs, such as cyclamen. Search for vine weevils at night by torchlight and kill if seen. Remove plants from pots to check for white grubs. Pick off any pests and remove as much old compost as possible from the plant; or drench with the systemic insecticide thiacloprid.

WHITEFLY

There are three types – cabbage, glasshouse and viburnum. These small, white insects and tiny, pale green nymphs suck sap from beneath leaves of ornamental and vegetable plants, especially members of the cabbage (Brassicaceae) and tomato (Solonaceae) families. Significant populations soon build throughout the year under glass, but only in summer outdoors. Cabbage whitefly is only of cosmetic concern, and is easily prevented by growing brassicas under fine mesh netting; the insecticides deltamethrin or lambda cyhalothrin can be used if necessary. Systemic insecticides acetamiprid and thiacloprid give good control of glasshouse and viburnum whitefly. Also use plant oils and fatty acids, but these require frequent application.

VINE WEEVIL

WHITEFLY

• DISEASES •

BOTRYTIS (GREY MOULD)

Symptoms of botrytis are: dead and dying plant material becoming covered in grey, fluffy mould; flowers developing brown flecks on petals; or young plants and seedlings collapsing. This disease is particularly prevalent in cool, humid conditions, such as found in glasshouses and conservatories over winter. Ventilate glasshouses, and water plants in the morning to prevent water pooling overnight. Also prevent an outbreak of botrytis by removing dead and dying plant material before infection can start.

POWDERY MILDEW

A white, powdery coating covers the surface of plant leaves and stems and infected tissue often becomes distorted or dies. Powdery mildew is particularly prevalent in dry conditions, and many leafy vegetable crops and fruit, including grapes (*Vitis*), are susceptible. Mulching and careful watering reduces plant stress and helps make them less prone to infection. Pick off and destroy infected leaves as soon as seen. Then spray them with a fungicide, such as myclobutanil or difenoconazole, or use plant and fish oil blends. Before applying, always check the suitability of the fungicide for use on fruit, vegetable and ornamental plants. Grow resistant species or cultivars when available.

176

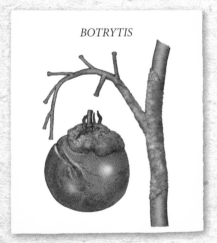

BOTRYTIS

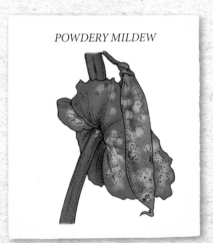

POWDERY MILDEW

RUSTS

A range of rust fungi mainly attack plant leaves, although flowers and fruit can be affected too. Pale spots appear on the leaf surfaces, before furry pustules form underneath; they are frequently orange-red in colour. Affected leaves often drop prematurely, and plant vigour is affected. Remove any fallen, infected leaves and destroy.

Some plants, such as snapdragons (*Antirrhinum*), can be killed by rusts, so grow resistant cultivars where possible. Spray plants with a fungicide, such as myclobutanil and triticonazole; use a copper-based one on some soft fruit crops and a liquid form of difenoconazole on some fruit and vegetable crops. Apply as soon as rust symptoms are noticed.

WILTING & LEAF FALL

Wilting is usually a symptom of water shortage, but if plants are wilting and the compost is moist this indicates there is a problem with plant roots. Check the compost is not waterlogged – drain plugs can become blocked. Having cleared the drainage holes, allow compost to dry. Keep plants healthy, use sterilised compost and do not overwater.

Continual wilting and leaf fall indicate root death and possible infection by a range of fungal diseases, such as phytophthora. Roots quickly become brown and shredded, and a V-shaped, black stain may appear at the stem base. There is no cure. Remove the plant and potting compost, and dispose of them. Do not add them to the compost heap.

177

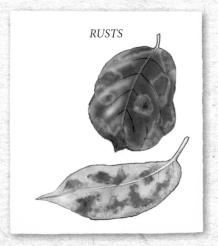

RUSTS

WILTING

• DIRECTORY OF SEASONAL TASKS •

MIDWINTER

Outdoors
- Provide frost protection for evergreens and tender plants.
- Shelter evergreens from cold, damaging winds.
- Last planting date for early summer bulbs, such as ornamental onions (*Allium*).
- Prune back flowering sideshoots of wisteria to two buds.

Indoors
- Plan planting displays, choose plants and decide whether to buy or raise from seed.
- Develop an integrated cropping plan for containerised vegetables, with successional sowings.
- Sow quick-maturing vegetables, such as radish and spring onions.
- Check overwintered plants for pests and diseases and pick off all dead or dying leaves and flowers.

LATE WINTER

Outdoors
- If the weather is good, plant out early sowings of hardy annuals and sweet peas (*Lathyrus odoratus*).
- Hard prune summer-flowering shrubs, such as buddleja.
- Hard prune summer-flowering and large-flowered clematis.

Indoors
- Sow perennials that flower in their first year from seed.
- Sow broad beans, peas and lettuce in slight heat for planting outdoors in late spring.
- Sow lobelias, using bottom heat (see Glossary, p184).

EARLY SPRING

Outdoors
- Repot or refresh the potting compost of evergreen trees and shrubs.
- Apply balanced, granular fertiliser to trees and shrubs.
- Prune out any winter-damaged growth on trees and shrubs.
- Direct sow early vegetables into containers and raised beds.
- Sow mixtures of hardy annuals in their final positions.
- Last planting opportunity for bare-roots trees, shrubs and fruit trees in containers.

Indoors
- Sow summer-flowering hardy annuals.
- Sow vegetables, such as tomatoes, sweet and chilli peppers and salad crops.
- Take softwood cuttings of overwintered bedding plants, such as fuchsia and pelargonium.
- Start to increase watering of winter-dormant cacti and succulents.

MIDSPRING

Outdoors
- Plant tender bulbs, such as dahlias, Indian shot plant (*Canna*) and arum lily (*Zantedeschia*).
- Stake and tie in annuals and climbing plants.

Indoors
- Last sowing of seed for summer annuals.
- Purchase bedding plants and grow on to required size.
- If warmth and good light are available, start to make up summer hanging baskets.
- Harden off and prepare hardier bedding plants for planting outdoors.
- Plant and support tomatoes and cucumbers in growing bags and other containers.
- Check all plants for first outbreaks of pests and diseases; treat as required.

LATE SPRING

Outdoors
- Remove spent flowerheads of spring-flowering bulbs. Lift and replant bulbs in nursery site as required.
- Plant out hardened, tender bedding plants after any danger of frost has passed.
- Stake and tie in annuals and climbing plants.
- Prune spring-flowering shrubs, removing spent flowerheads and weak, thin shoots.
- Feed young ornamental and vegetable plants with nitrogen-rich liquid fertiliser.

Indoors
- Grow on hardy and half-hardy plants.
- Plant and support aubergines, sweet and chilli peppers in growing bags and other containers.
- Plant up windowboxes with summer bedding and transfer outdoors after the danger of frost has passed.

EARLY SUMMER

Outdoors
- Continue to plant out tender bedding.
- Finish off pruning spring-flowering shrubs.
- Provide support and tie in tall, summer-flowering annuals, perennials and climbers.
- Feed developing ornamental and vegetable plants, changing to high-potash, liquid fertiliser as flowers form.
- Sow successional crops of vegetables and salad greens after harvesting your first sowings.
- Apply balanced liquid fertiliser to all container-grown plants as growth ensues.

Indoors
- Plant out tender vegetables, such as cucumbers and courgettes.
- Remove sideshoots of tomatoes and cucumbers and tie growths to supporting structures.
- Keep long-term plantings of trees, shrubs and conifers thoroughly watered.

MIDSUMMER

Outdoors
- Continue to apply high-potash, liquid fertiliser to ornamental plants and fruiting crops; give nitrogen fertiliser to salad greens.
- Remove spent flowers of early summer bedding and sweet peas to encourage more flowers to form.
- Start planting autumn-flowering crocus, colchicum and sowbread (Cyclamen).

Indoors
- Sow bedding plants for spring display, such as wallflowers (*Erysimum*), pansies (*Viola* × *wittrockiana*), daisies (*Bellis*) and forget-me-nots (*Myosotis*). Keep plants out of hot sun.

LATE SUMMER

Outdoors
- Summer-prune wisteria in containers.
- Collect seed of annuals (except F1 hybrids) for resowing next year.
- Keep all containers well watered and apply liquid feed as required.

Indoors
- Sow hardy annuals and sweet peas for early flowering.
- Sow seeds or take cuttings of pelargonium to be overwintered for an early display.
- Pot up bulbs being forced for winter displays.

EARLY AUTUMN

Outdoors
- Purchase and plant spring bedding, such as pansies and forget-me-nots.
- Plant spring-flowering bulbs, such as snowdrops (*Galanthus*), daffodils (*Narcissus*), scilla, tulips (*Tulipa*) and hyacinths (*Hyacinthus*).
- Plant early summer bulbs, such as ornamental onions.
- Plant up winter and spring displays.

Indoors
- Prick out and grow on early sowings of sweet peas and hardy annuals in pots.
- Take cuttings of bedding to be overwintered as rooted plantlets.
- Sow containers or beds with cut-and-come-again salads for winter cropping.
- Plant up containers with strawberries for forcing an early crop.

MIDAUTUMN

Outdoors
- Lift and dry off tender bulbs such as Indian shot plant and dahlia.
- Cut back and lift perennial bedding plants for overwintering under glass.
- Plant evergreens in containers.
- Complete planting of spring-flowering bulbs.
- Repot or pot on fruit trees.

Indoors
- Pick last fruit from tomatoes, cucumbers, chilli and sweet peppers.
- Remove growing bags and empty containers of spent crop plants and potting composts.
- Purchase materials to provide winter protection for vulnerable plants.

LATE AUTUMN

Outdoors
- Last opportunity for successfully planting tulips.
- Remove spent plants and potting compost from containers and put on compost heap.
- Clean and scrub pots to remove debris, which could harbour pests and diseases.
- Move planted pots to more sheltered positions and raise them off the ground to prevent waterlogging.
- Mulch roots and cover or insulate stems and growth points of tender plants against hard frost.
- Start to plant bare-root trees and shrubs between now and early spring.

Indoors
- If warm, empty the glasshouse and wash the superstructure and staging, to control pests and diseases.
- Continue to bring in and store bedding plants being overwintered.

A regiment of potted bulbs awakens in readiness to produce a succession of blossom throughout winter and spring.

EARLY WINTER

Outdoors

- Construct shelters and windbreaks to protect evergreens and conifers against scorching, winter wind.
- Position containers with winter interest near windows and entrances for maximum impact.
- Remove snow from shrubs and other weak-stemmed plants to prevent its weight from snapping shoots.

Indoors

- Heat the glasshouse to maintain frost-free conditions as required.
- Ventilate the glasshouse on warm days to improve air circulation.
- Pick over plants, removing dead or diseased foliage to control spread of diseases such as botrytis (grey mould).

• GLOSSARY •

Acid Term applied to potting compost or garden soil with a pH of below 7.

Alkaline Term applied to potting compost or garden soil with a pH over 7.

Annual Plant that completes its life cycle within one growing season.

Bare-root plant A plant, usually a perennial, tree or shrub, lifted, generally while dormant , with very little or no soil around its roots.

Bedding plant Ornamental plant used for temporary garden display, usually in spring or summer.

Biennial Plant that completes its life cycle within two growing seasons.

Bottom heat Warmth, usually provided artificially via heating cables in a propagator or glasshouse bench, to encourage the development of roots in cuttings or the germination of seeds, particularly in cold weather.

Broadcast sowing Seeds sown over an area of soil or potting compost, rather than in lines (drills).

Bulb Underground storage organ consisting of layers of swollen, fleshy leaves or leaf bases enclosing a growth bud.

Cold frame A timber or brick box, with hinged, glazed lid sited outdoors. Used

for hardening off plants, providing protection in winter or increasing soil temperature for germinating seeds or raising cuttings in cold weather.

Compost, garden Decayed organic matter used to improve the condition and fertility of soil or to act as a mulch.

Compost, seed and potting Mixtures of rotted greenwaste, wood fibre, coir, sand, loam, peat and other additives used for growing and raising plants.

Coir Pulverised coconut husk, often used in potting composts.

Corm Solid, swollen stem base, resembling a bulb and acting as a storage organ.

Cotyledon Seed leaf, usually the first to emerge.

Cultivar A plant raised and named in cultivation for its particular qualities, rather than a botanical variety.

Current year's growth Shoots grown from buds during the present growing season.

Cutting Separated piece of stem, root or leaf selected in order to propagate a new plant. Stem cuttings can be softwood (fresh, young growth), semiripe (tougher, maturing growth) or hardwood (mature, woody growth).

Damping off Diseases that kill seedlings soon after germination.

Ericaceous Plants belonging to the heather family (Ericaceae) requiring acid soil conditions. Any acid-loving plant is usually referred to as being ericaceous, whether it is in the Ericaceae family or not.

Family taxonomic category containing one or more genera.

Family tree Fruit trees grafted with a number of compatible cultivars.

Fertiliser Range of organic and inorganic substances used to feed plants.

Genus (pl. **Genera**) A group (or groups) of allied species in botanical classification.

Germination Development of a dormant seed into a seedling.

Grafted plant Method of propagation fusing two plant parts together, often to improve performance. Top part is termed the scion; bottom, the rootstock.

Growing bag Plastic sacks of growing media in which plants are grown.

Growing point Tips of roots or shoots from which new growth forms.

Half-hardy Plant unable to survive cold winter or spring conditions without protection, but not requiring protection year-round.

Harden off The acclimatisation of plants growing in warmth to colder conditions, usually outdoors.

Hardy Plant capable of surviving winter outdoors without protection.

Heritage varieties Old cultivars, usually of vegetables or fruit, grown for their particular characteristics.

John Innes compost Trustworthy standardised recipes for loam-based potting composts.

Lateral Bud or shoot emanating from the stem, rather than top or base.

Leader Central, vertical, dominant shoot.

185

Liquid feed Fertiliser concentrate in either crystalline or liquid form, diluted before use.

Mulch Substances, usually organic or mineral, placed around plants to insulate against cold temperatures, retain moisture or help prevent weed growth.

Perennial Plant living for at least three seasons.

Perlite Neutral, sterile and porous, granular, white mineral used in some potting composts or as a compost additive.

pH Scientific scale 1–14, denoting acidity (below 7) or alkalinity (above 7); neutral is 7.

Pinching Removal of the main growing tips to encourage sideshoots to form.

Plug plant Young plants sown and/or raised in moulded trays containing plugs of potting compost.

Plunge Bury plants in containers up to the rim in a bed or border.

Pot-bound Plant condition reached when roots fill the pot and exhaust the available nutrients.

Potting off Transferring a small plantlet or seedling into the first container.

Potting on Transferring a plant from its current container into a larger one.

Pricking out Transplanting individual young seedlings to provide them with more space to grow larger.

Propagator A box, often heated, with a transparent lid, in which to germinate seeds or root cuttings.

Repotting Using fresh potting compost to replace stale or depleted compost of established potted plants.

Seed leaf *see* Cotyledon.

Space sowing Seeds sown individually or at prescribed distances apart.

Spur Woody branch system that carries flowers and eventually fruits.

Succulent Plant adapted to living in arid conditions by storing water in its thick, fleshy leaves and stems.

Thin or thinning out Reducing the numbers of seedlings, buds, flowers, fruits or branches.

Topdressing Material such as organic matter or fertiliser applied to the surface of garden soil or potting compost without being dug in.

Trained fruit Trees pruned and shaped to reduce size, enhance ripening and yield, particularly for wall culture. Styles include fans, espalier (tiered branches) and cordons (slanted trunk).

Tuber Swollen underground stem or root acting as a storage organ against cold and/or arid conditions.

Vermiculite Lightweight, sterile, moisture- and nutrient-absorbing clay mineral used in potting composts, particularly for propagation.

Watering in Applying water to seedbeds or to freshly potted seedlings or established plants.

Potted displays of plants are an essential part of the garden scene, providing freedom to decorate and embellish it in exciting and creative ways.

• PICTURE CREDITS •

Note The acknowledgements below appear in source order.

GAP Photos BBC Magazines Ltd 146, 155, BBC Magazines Ltd/design Malcolm Miller 96; Carol Casselde 136; Clive Nichols/locatio Feibusch Garden, San Francisco 105; Dianna Jazwinski 102; Elke Borkowski 36, 140; FhF Greenmedia 165; Fiona Lea 99; Friedrich Strauss 38, 47, 53 r, 61, 67, 69 l, 95, 111 l, 133, 135, 148; Gary Smith 10-11, 51, 58; Geoff Kidd 59; Graham Strong 52. 75, 141, 169; Janet Johnson 144; John Glover 101, 123, John Glover/design Peter Reid 108; John Glover/location The Oast Houses, Hampshire 64-5; Jonathan Buckley/design Sarah Raven; Perch Hill 22-3; Julia Boulton 30; Lynn Keddie 120-1; Mark Winwood 81, 139; Michael Howes 161; Rob Whitworth 24, Rob Whitworth/design Heather Culpan & Nicola Reed 44; Ron Evans 89; S & O Mathews 98 l; Suzie Gibbons 158; Tim Gainey 2, 43

Garden Collection Andrew Lawson/Eastgrove Cottage, Hereford 66; Liz Eddison 57, Liz Eddison/Whichford Pottery 91; Nicola Stocken Tomkins 183, 187

Garden World Images Françoise Davis 63; Gary Smith 40

Helen Griffin 151

Octopus Publishing Group Torie Chugg 41; Will Heap 8

RHS Images 85, 149; Carol Sheppard 83; Neil Hepworth 42, 77, 82, 88; Philippa Gibson 98 r; Suzanne Drew 98 c; Tim Sandall 14, 15, 29, 32, 53 l, 68, 71, 72, 73, 74, 79, 80, 87, 92, 94, 107, 111 r, 113, 118, 119, 157

The Garden Tim Sandall 7, 21, 49

Thinkstock Dorling Kindersley RF 54; Hemera 145; iStockphoto 9, 12, 17, 18 l & r 18, 19, 20, 35, 48, 55, 62, 69 r, 76, 109, 124, 126, 127, 129, 142, 143, 147, 162, 163, 164, 166, 171; Photodisc 122